TAKING ON THE B.E.S.T

MW01172745

3RD GRADE MATH

STUDENT WORKBOOK

A high-energy math program aligned specifically to Florida's B.E.S.T. Standards for Math

Video Lessons with Ms. McCarthy

Extra Practice to Promote Student Growth

Math Tasks, Error Analysis & More

Created by Sarah McCarthy

HEY WORLD CHANGER!

I just wanted to take a moment to introduce myself. My name is Ms. McCarthy, and I am so excited to be a part of your math journey this year. My mission is to make math FUN, make it CLICK, and make it STICK for you. I will be there to support you by walking you through the skills and tools you will need to be successful in math this year, but that will only take you so far.

You see, your willingness to try and persistence to keep going even when it gets tough will be the keys to your success. I challenge you to take charge of your learning and stick with each math skill until you get it. Think you can handle that? I believe in you and know that you can do this!

Go ahead and commit to learning and growing this year by filling out the statement below:

I, _____, hereby make a sincere commitment to give this school year everything I've got. I will take charge of my learning by asking questions and solving problems to the best of my ability. When work is challenging for me, I will stay determined and stick with it until I get it.

Sign your name: X _____

Way to go! Let's get to it, and "LET ME TEACH YA!"

− Ms. McCarthy

1

© McCarthy Math Academy

"TAKING ON THE B.E.S.T."
Theme Song

Do you know what the BEST version of you looks like?
Just take a look in the mirror,
The person that you were born to be and say,
"I'M TAKING ON THE BEST!"

Every day is a new day to step it up
And maybe some days I feel like giving up
I just don't get it,
but I can't forget
That I'm a believer in the POWER OF YET!

I may not know it now, but I will
Take a deep breath, and I'm chill
Mistakes are part of the game,
I embrace 'em
I don't run from my fears,
I face 'em

How?
I pay attention
I take charge of my learning
Draw it out, and work it out
To show my journey
Try until it clicks,
Make sure that it sticks,
Working at it constantly is my secret

Practice is not something I do once I'm good
It's the one thing I do that makes me good
So I take another step
I'm obsessed with progress
You know why? (Why?)
I'M TAKING ON THE BEST!

© McCarthy Math Academy

MATHEMATICAL
Mindset Creed

THIS IS A SAFE PLACE TO MAKE MISTAKES.
Mistakes help me learn and grow.

I AM A HARD WORKER.
I stick with it until I get it.

I AM BRAVE. I TAKE CHARGE OF MY LEARNING.
I ask questions when I don't understand.

WHEN IN DOUBT, I DRAW IT OUT (IF POSSIBLE).
And it's always possible to work it out.

I RESPECT AND ACTIVELY LISTEN
To the ideas of others.

NOTES

_____

_____

_____

_____

_____

_____

_____

TABLE OF CONTENTS

Video lessons can only be viewed with a membership at McCarthyMathAcademy.com

© McCarthy Math Academy

TABLE OF CONTENTS

Video lessons can only be viewed with a membership at McCarthyMathAcademy.com

© McCarthy Math Academy

TABLE OF CONTENTS

(MA.5.NSO.2.2 continues on next page)

Video lessons can only be viewed with a membership at McCarthyMathAcademy.com

© McCarthy Math Academy

TABLE OF CONTENTS

(MA.5.NSO.2.4 continues on next page)

Video lessons can only be viewed with a membership at McCarthyMathAcademy.com

© McCarthy Math Academy

TABLE OF CONTENTS

(MA.3.FR.1.2 continues on next page)

Video lessons can only be viewed with a membership at McCarthyMathAcademy.com

© McCarthy Math Academy

TABLE OF CONTENTS

(MA.3.FR.2.1 continues on next page)

Video lessons can only be viewed with a membership at McCarthyMathAcademy.com

© McCarthy Math Academy

TABLE OF CONTENTS

(MA.3.AR.1.1 continues on next page)

Video lessons can only be viewed with a membership at McCarthyMathAcademy.com

© McCarthy Math Academy

TABLE OF CONTENTS

(MA.3.AR.2.1 continues on next page)

Video lessons can only be viewed with a membership at McCarthyMathAcademy.com

© McCarthy Math Academy

TABLE OF CONTENTS

Video lessons can only be viewed with a membership at McCarthyMathAcademy.com

© McCarthy Math Academy

TABLE OF CONTENTS

Video lessons can only be viewed with a membership at McCarthyMathAcademy.com

© McCarthy Math Academy

TABLE OF CONTENTS

(MA.3.M.2.1 continues on next page)

Video lessons can only be viewed with a membership at McCarthyMathAcademy.com

© McCarthy Math Academy

TABLE OF CONTENTS

(MA.3.GR.1.1 continues on next page)

＊Video lessons can only be viewed with a membership at McCarthyMathAcademy.com＊

© McCarthy Math Academy

TABLE OF CONTENTS

(MA.3.GR.1.3 continues on next page)

Video lessons can only be viewed with a membership at McCarthyMathAcademy.com

© McCarthy Math Academy

TABLE OF CONTENTS

© McCarthy Math Academy

TABLE OF CONTENTS

Video lessons can only be viewed with a membership at McCarthyMathAcademy.com

© McCarthy Math Academy

TABLE OF CONTENTS

© McCarthy Math Academy

PLACE VALUE

9 , 3 0 8

VALUE OF DIGITS

7 , 0 7 7

© McCarthy Math Academy

STANDARD FORM	3,256
WORD FORM	
EXPANDED FORM	

STANDARD FORM	
WORD FORM	
EXPANDED FORM	7,000 + 900 + 4

© McCarthy Math Academy

TAKING ON THE B.E.S.T.

| Extra Practice #I | Reading and Writing Numbers (Standard Form to Word Form)

Fill in the blank spaces in the tables below.

1

STANDARD FORM	876
WORD FORM	

2

STANDARD FORM	
WORD FORM	one hundred two

3

STANDARD FORM	5,039
WORD FORM	

4

STANDARD FORM	
WORD FORM	nine thousand, three hundred thirty-three

5

STANDARD FORM	
WORD FORM	four thousand, seven hundred sixty-six

© McCarthy Math Academy

TAKING ON THE B.E.S.T.

Fill in the blank spaces in the tables below.

1

STANDARD FORM	297
EXPANDED FORM	

2

STANDARD FORM	
EXPANDED FORM	6,000 + 90 + 3

3

STANDARD FORM	5,039
EXPANDED FORM	

4

STANDARD FORM	
EXPANDED FORM	800 70 + 1 ————

TAKING ON THE B.E.S.T.

Fill in the blank spaces in the tables below.

1

STANDARD FORM	
EXPANDED FORM	
WORD FORM	**Five thousand, fifty**

2

STANDARD FORM	
EXPANDED FORM	**8,000 + 100 + 2**
WORD FORM	

3

STANDARD FORM	**2,009**
EXPANDED FORM	
WORD FORM	

4

STANDARD FORM	
EXPANDED FORM	**3,000 + 700**
WORD FORM	

TAKING ON THE B.E.S.T.

PART ONE

Derek pays his cell phone bill by mailing in a check. Derek needs help filling out the word form of the amount on the check. Please show him how to do this.

[Hint: $127.00 is equal to $127.]

```
                                                      0515
Your
Name _____
                                    Date_____

Pay to the    Cell Phone Company          $ | 127.00 |
Order of   _____

           _____ and 00/100  Dollars
       ↰  (Write word form here)

Memo  September bill          Derek Franklin
     _____  _____

:032106      :052713090616      :853012
```

PART TWO

Derek says that 127 written in expanded form is 100 + 200 + 7. Do you agree with Derek? Explain your thinking.

_____

_____

_____

_____

TAKING ON THE B.E.S.T.

Math Misconception Mystery
(PAGE 1)

BEFORE THE VIDEO: Solve the problem on your own.

Write 5,000 + 30 + 8 in word form.

DURING THE VIDEO: Pause after each "character" solves the problem and jot down quick notes to help you remember what they did correctly or incorrectly.

Character #1 _____

Character #2 _____

Character #3 _____

Character #4 _____

© McCarthy Math Academy

TAKING ON THE B.E.S.T.

Math Misconception Mystery
(PAGE 2)

AFTER THE VIDEO: Discuss and analyze their answers.

The most reasonable answer belongs to Character # _____ because

_____

_____

_____

_____

(Justify how this character's work makes sense.)

Let's help the others:			
	Character #___:	Character #___:	Character #___:
What did this character do that was correct?			
Identify their error			
What do they need to know to understand for next time?			

TAKING ON THE B.E.S.T.

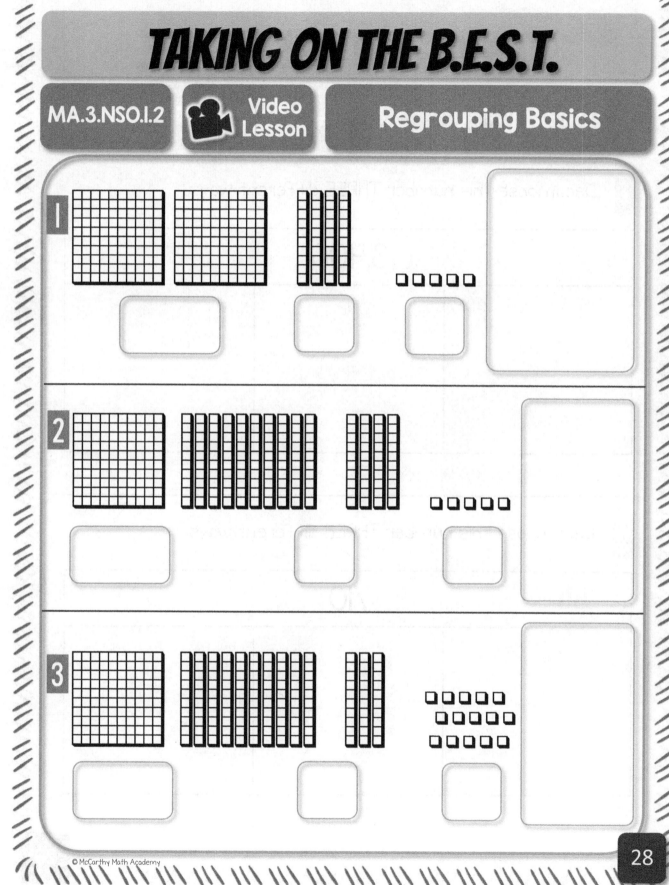

1.

2.

3.

© McCarthy Math Academy

TAKING ON THE B.E.S.T.

1 Decompose this number THREE different ways.

3,406		

2 Decompose this number THREE different ways.

710		

© McCarthy Math Academy

TAKING ON THE B.E.S.T.

Extra Practice #1

Decomposing Numbers #1

1 Which of the following shows a way to decompose 5,432?
- Ⓐ 5 thousands + 43 hundreds + 2 ones
- Ⓑ 5 thousands + 4 hundreds + 32 tens
- Ⓒ 54 hundreds + 32 tens
- Ⓓ 54 hundreds + 32 ones

2 Which of the following shows a way to decompose 1,079?
- Ⓐ 10 hundreds + 7 tens + 9 ones
- Ⓑ 10 hundreds + 79 tens
- Ⓒ 1 thousand + 79 tens
- Ⓓ 1 thousand + 7 hundreds + 9 ones

3 Which of the following shows a way to decompose 3,960?
- Ⓐ 3 thousands + 9 hundreds + 60 tens
- Ⓑ 39 hundreds + 60 ones
- Ⓒ 396 tens + 60 ones
- Ⓓ 396 ones

© McCarthy Math Academy

1 Select all of the ways to decompose 874.
- (A) 8 hundreds + 7 tens + 4 ones
- (B) 87 hundreds + 4 ones
- (C) 87 tens + 4 ones
- (D) 874 ones
- (E) 874 tens

2 Select all of the ways to decompose 2,032.
- (A) 203 tens + 2 ones
- (B) 20 hundreds + 30 tens + 2 ones
- (C) 2 thousands + 3 hundreds + 2 ones
- (D) 20 hundreds + 3 tens + 2 ones
- (E) 2 thousands + 30 tens + 2 ones

3 Select all of the ways to decompose 1,456.
- (A) 14 hundreds + 56 ones
- (B) 14 hundreds + 50 tens + 6 ones
- (C) 1 thousand + 456 ones
- (D) 1 thousand + 45 tens + 6 ones
- (E) 145 hundreds + 6 ones

TAKING ON THE B.E.S.T.

1 Decompose this number THREE different ways by regrouping at least one digit.

3,406		

2 Decompose this number THREE different ways by regrouping at least one digit.

899		

TAKING ON THE B.E.S.T.

1 Which of the following shows a way to decompose 6,027?
- Ⓐ 5 thousands + 102 tens + 7 ones
- Ⓑ 5 thousands + 2 tens + 17 ones
- Ⓒ 6 thousands + 12 hundreds + 7 ones
- Ⓓ 6 thousands + 2 tens + 17 ones

2 Which of the following shows a way to decompose 2,243?
- Ⓐ 2 thousands + 1 hundred + 53 ones
- Ⓑ 2 thousands + 1 hundred + 153 ones
- Ⓒ 1 thousand + 11 hundreds + 43 ones
- Ⓓ 1 thousand + 11 hundreds + 143 ones

3 Which of the following shows a way to decompose 7,815?
- Ⓐ 6 thousands + 18 hundreds + 15 tens
- Ⓑ 6 thousands + 8 hundreds + 25 ones
- Ⓒ 7 thousands + 7 hundreds + 11 tens + 5 ones
- Ⓓ 7 thousands + 8 hundreds + 11 tens + 5 ones

© McCarthy Math Academy

TAKING ON THE B.E.S.T.

1 Select all of the ways to decompose 513.
- (A) 4 hundreds + 10 tens + 13 ones
- (B) 4 hundreds + 11 tens + 3 ones
- (C) 5 hundreds + 1 ten + 3 ones
- (D) 5 hundreds + 11 tens + 3 ones
- (E) 5 hundreds + 11 tens + 13 ones

2 Select all of the ways to decompose 3,559.
- (A) 2 thousands + 5 hundreds + 15 tens + 9 ones
- (B) 2 thousands + 15 hundreds + 4 tens + 19 ones
- (C) 34 hundreds + 15 tens + 9 ones
- (D) 34 hundreds + 15 tens + 59 ones
- (E) 3 thousands + 54 tens + 19 ones

3 Select all of the ways to decompose 6,427.
- (A) 5 thousands + 4 hundreds + 37 ones
- (B) 5 thousands + 141 tens + 17 ones
- (C) 5 thousands + 14 hundreds + 17 ones
- (D) 6 thousands + 42 tens + 7 ones
- (E) 6 thousands + 42 hundreds + 7 ones

© McCarthy Math Academy

TAKING ON THE B.E.S.T.

1 Compose the amounts to find the value of the expression.

73 hundreds + 28 ones

2 Compose the amounts to find the value of the expression.

6 thousands + 11 tens + 4 ones

TAKING ON THE B.E.S.T.

1 Compose the amounts to find the value of the expression.

16 hundreds + 42 ones

2 Compose the amounts to find the value of the expression.

3 thousands + 19 tens + 3 ones

© McCarthy Math Academy

TAKING ON THE B.E.S.T.

| **Math Missions** | **Composing and Decomposing Numbers**

Use the number 1,862 to complete the following tasks.

PART ONE

Express the number using only **hundreds** and **ones**. Model with a drawing.

PART TWO

Express the number using only **thousands, tens and ones**. Model with a drawing.

TAKING ON THE B.E.S.T.

Math Misconception Mystery (PAGE 1)

BEFORE THE VIDEO: Solve the problem on your own.

Express the number 2,438 using only tens and ones.

DURING THE VIDEO: Pause after each "character" solves the problem and jot down quick notes to help you remember what they did correctly or incorrectly.

Character #1 _____

Character #2 _____

Character #3 _____

Character #4 _____

© McCarthy Math Academy

TAKING ON THE B.E.S.T.

Math Misconception Mystery
(PAGE 2)

AFTER THE VIDEO: Discuss and analyze their answers.

The most reasonable answer belongs to Character # _____ because

_____

_____

_____

_____

(Justify how this character's work makes sense.)

Let's help the others:

	Character #___:	Character #___:	Character #___:
What did this character do that was correct?			
Identify their error			
What do they need to know to understand for next time?			

© McCarthy Math Academy

TAKING ON THE B.E.S.T.

MA.3.NSO.I.3  **Video Lesson** | **Comparing Two Numbers Using Place Value Blocks**

1 Compare 543 and 534 using place value blocks.

2 Compare 2,716 and 2,671 using place value blocks.

3 Compare 1,809 and 1,809 using place value blocks.

© McCarthy Math Academy

TAKING ON THE B.E.S.T.

1 Compare 148 and 184 using place value blocks.

2 Compare 716 and 716 using place value blocks.

3 Compare 1,312 and 1,213 using place value blocks.

© McCarthy Math Academy

TAKING ON THE B.E.S.T.

1 Compare 469 and 496 using place value.

2 Compare 3,408 and 3,408 using place value.

3 Compare 1,414 and 4,141 using place value.

© McCarthy Math Academy

1 Compare 344 and 433 using place value.

2 Compare 1,234 and 1,233 using place value.

3 Compare 2,384 and 2,391 using place value.

TAKING ON THE B.E.S.T.

1 Compare 155 and 55 using the number line.

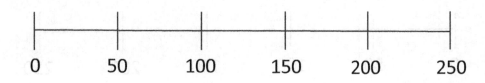

0   50   100   150   200   250

2 Compare 281 and 302 using the number line below.

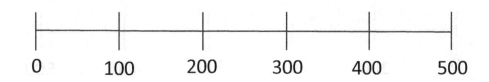

0   100   200   300   400   500

3 Compare 5,084 and 5,840 using the number line below.

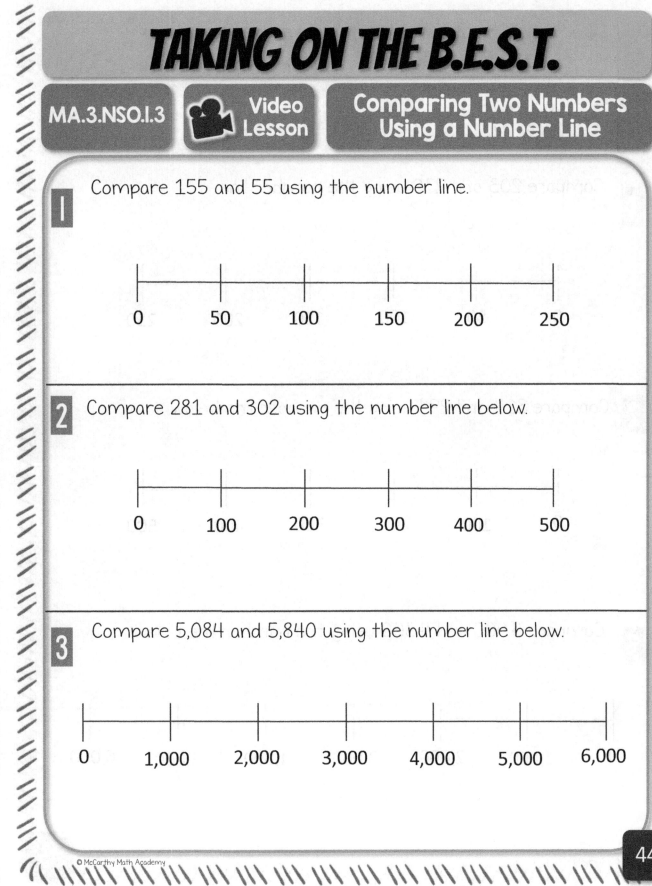

0   1,000   2,000   3,000   4,000   5,000   6,000

© McCarthy Math Academy

TAKING ON THE B.E.S.T.

1 Compare 203 and 230 using the number line.

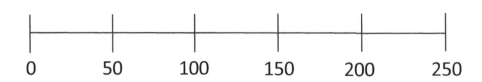

```
|----+----+----+----+----+----|
0    50   100  150  200  250
```

2 Compare 314 and 294 using the number line below.

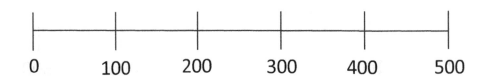

```
|----+----+----+----+----+----|
0   100  200  300  400  500
```

3 Compare 4,900 and 4,300 using the number line below.

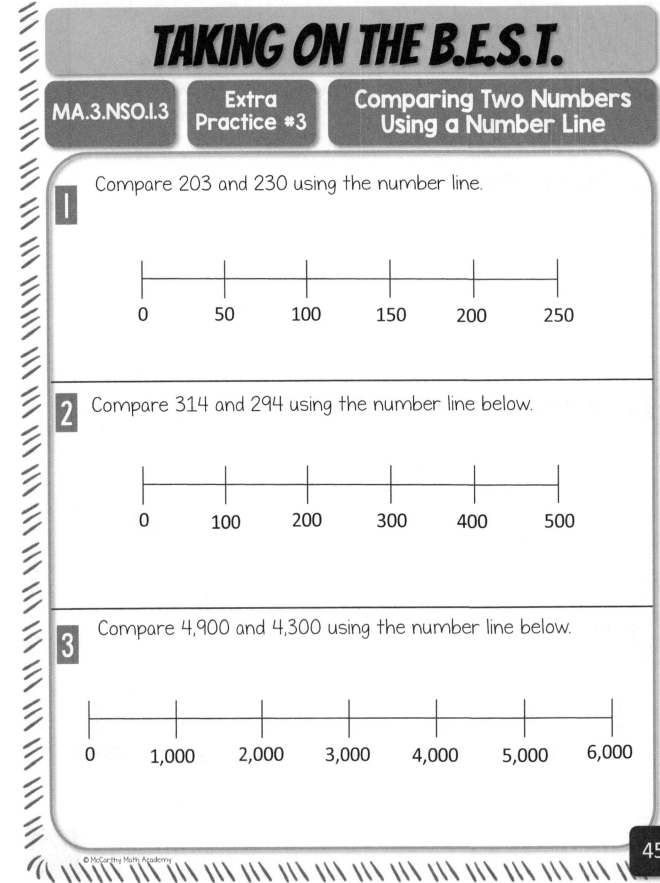

```
|----+----+----+----+----+----|
0  1,000 2,000 3,000 4,000 5,000 6,000
```

© McCarthy Math Academy

TAKING ON THE B.E.S.T.

  **Video Lesson** **Plot and Order Numbers Using a Number Line**

1 Plot the numbers to order them from LEAST to GREATEST:

123; 132; 89

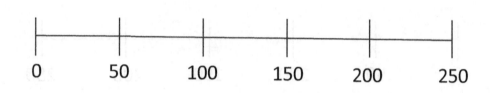

2 Plot the numbers to order them from LEAST to GREATEST.

505; 450; 493; 542

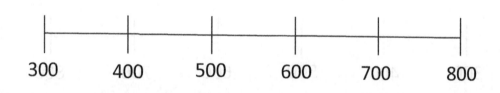

3 Plot the numbers to order them from GREATEST to LEAST.

6,890; 6,991; 5,814; 7,007

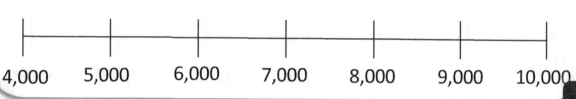

© McCarthy Math Academy

TAKING ON THE B.E.S.T.

1 Plot the numbers to order them from LEAST to GREATEST:

185; 203; 57

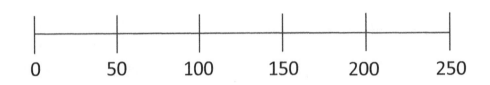

2 Plot the numbers to order them from LEAST to GREATEST.

380; 730; 680

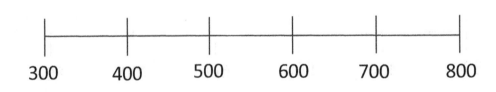

3 Plot the numbers to order them from GREATEST to LEAST.

5,225; 5,522; 7,013; 8,915

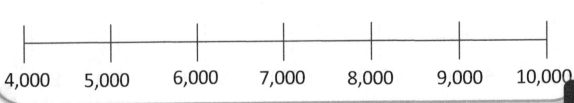

TAKING ON THE B.E.S.T.

MA.3.NSO.1.3 | **Math Missions** | **Plot, Compare, and Order Numbers**

PART ONE

Use the cards below to create three different numbers. The digit in the thousands place has been given.

CARDS

6 0 5

3, ☐ ☐ ☐

3, ☐ ☐ ☐

3, ☐ ☐ ☐

PART TWO

Arrange the numbers in ascending order (least to greatest). Use BOTH place value strategies and a number line to explain your thinking.

```
|-------|-------|-------|-------|-------|-------|-------|
3,000   3,100   3,200   3,300   3,400   3,500   3,600   3,700
```

_____

_____

_____

_____

TAKING ON THE B.E.S.T.

Math Misconception Mystery (PAGE 1)

BEFORE THE VIDEO: Solve the problem on your own.

> Use <, >, or = to correctly compare 9,166 and 9,661. Justify your comparison using place value.

DURING THE VIDEO: Pause after each "character" solves the problem and jot down quick notes to help you remember what they did correctly or incorrectly.

Character #1 _____	Character #2 _____
Character #3 _____	Character #4 _____

© McCarthy Math Academy

TAKING ON THE B.E.S.T.

Math Misconception Mystery (PAGE 2)

AFTER THE VIDEO: Discuss and analyze their answers.

The most reasonable answer belongs to Character # _____ because

_____

_____

_____

_____

(Justify how this character's work makes sense.)

Let's help the others:

	Character #___:	Character #___:	Character #___:
What did this character do that was correct?			
Identify their error			
What do they need to know to understand for next time?			

© McCarthy Math Academy

TAKING ON THE B.E.S.T.

 **Video Lesson**

Round to the Nearest Ten

1 Round 314 to the nearest ten. Use a number line, place value blocks, and a place value chart to show your thinking.

2 Round 257 to the nearest ten. Use a number line, place value blocks, and a place value chart to show your thinking.

3 Round 135 to the nearest ten. Use a number line, place value blocks, and a place value chart to show your thinking.

© McCarthy Math Academy

TAKING ON THE B.E.S.T.

1 Round 233 to the nearest ten. Use a number line, place value blocks, OR a place value chart to show your thinking.

2 Round 867 to the nearest ten. Use a number line, place value blocks, OR a place value chart to show your thinking.

3 Round 655 to the nearest ten. Use a number line, place value blocks, OR a place value chart to show your thinking

TAKING ON THE B.E.S.T.

MA.3.NSO.1.4 | **Extra Practice #2** | **Round to the Nearest Ten**

1 Round 476 to the nearest ten. Use a number line, place value blocks, OR a place value chart to show your thinking.

2 Round 481 to the nearest ten. Use a number line, place value blocks, OR a place value chart to show your thinking.

3 Round 485 to the nearest ten. Use a number line, place value blocks, OR a place value chart to show your thinking

© McCarthy Math Academy

53

TAKING ON THE B.E.S.T.

  **Video Lesson** | **Round to the Nearest Hundred**

1 Round 314 to the nearest hundred. Use a number line, place value blocks, and a place value chart to show your thinking.

2 Round 257 to the nearest hundred. Use a number line, place value blocks, and a place value chart to show your thinking.

3 Round 135 to the nearest hundred. Use a number line, place value blocks, and a place value chart to show your thinking.

TAKING ON THE B.E.S.T.

1 Round 233 to the nearest hundred. Use a number line, place value blocks, OR a place value chart to show your thinking.

2 Round 867 to the nearest hundred. Use a number line, place value blocks, OR a place value chart to show your thinking.

3 Round 655 to the nearest hundred. Use a number line, place value blocks, OR a place value chart to show your thinking.

TAKING ON THE B.E.S.T.

1 Round 476 to the nearest hundred. Use a number line, place value blocks, OR a place value chart to show your thinking.

2 Round 349 to the nearest hundred. Use a number line, place value blocks, OR a place value chart to show your thinking.

3 Round 968 to the nearest hundred. Use a number line, place value blocks, OR a place value chart to show your thinking.

TAKING ON THE B.E.S.T.

  **Video Lesson** | **Estimating Sums and Differences**

1 Use rounding to estimate the sum of 234 and 471.

2 Use rounding to estimate the difference of 182 from 713.

3 Use rounding to estimate the sum of 828 and 512. Then, estimate the difference of 512 from 828.

© McCarthy Math Academy

57

TAKING ON THE B.E.S.T.

1 Use rounding to estimate the sum of 871 and 123.

2 Use rounding to estimate the difference of 615 from 950.

3 Use rounding to estimate the sum of 977 and 673. Then, estimate the difference of 673 from 977.

1 Use rounding to estimate the sum of 745 and 219.

2 Use rounding to estimate the difference of 364 from 1,000.

3 Use rounding to estimate the sum of 318 and 599. Then, estimate the difference of 318 from 599.

© McCarthy Math Academy

TAKING ON THE B.E.S.T.

| MA.3.NSO.1.4 | Math Mission | Rounding to the Nearest Ten and Hundred |

PART ONE

Use the cards below to create three different numbers. Then, round the numbers that you create to the nearest ten and hundred.

CARDS

| 7 | 2 | 5 |

Round to the Nearest 10	Round to the Nearest 100

PART TWO

Tosha creates a number using the same cards. Her number rounded to the nearest ten is 530. Her number rounded to the nearest hundred is 500. What is the number that Tosha creates from the cards? Explain your thinking.

_____

_____

_____

_____

© McCarthy Math Academy

TAKING ON THE B.E.S.T.

Math Misconception Mystery
(PAGE I)

BEFORE THE VIDEO: Solve the problem on your own.

Ellie has $283 in her savings account. Round this amount to the nearest ten and hundred.

DURING THE VIDEO: Pause after each "character" solves the problem and jot down quick notes to help you remember what they did correctly or incorrectly.

Character #1 _____

Character #2 _____

Character #3 _____

Character #4 _____

© McCarthy Math Academy

61

TAKING ON THE B.E.S.T.

Math Misconception Mystery (PAGE 2)

AFTER THE VIDEO: Discuss and analyze their answers.

The most reasonable answer belongs to Character # _____ because

_____

_____

_____

_____

(Justify how this character's work makes sense.)

Let's help the others:

	Character #___:	Character #___:	Character #___:
What did this character do that was correct?			
Identify their error			
What do they need to know to understand for next time?			

© McCarthy Math Academy

What is addition?

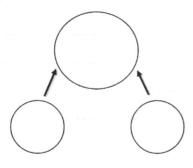

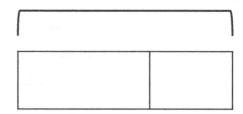

2 Gerri counts 1,783 jellybeans in a bag. Her brother, Hector, gives her another 365 jellybeans. How many jellybeans does she have now? Estimate, then determine the exact amount.

3 Iniya takes 894 pictures on Monday. The next day, she takes 196 pictures. How many pictures does she take over the span of two days? Estimate, then determine the exact amount.

TAKING ON THE B.E.S.T.

1 Use rounding to estimate the sum of 918 and 135. Then, find the exact sum.

2 Use rounding to estimate the sum of 858 and 1,002. Then find the exact sum.

3 Use rounding to estimate the sum of 344 and 8,784. Then find the exact sum.

TAKING ON THE B.E.S.T.

1 Use rounding to estimate the sum of 3,473 and 7,882. Then, find the exact sum.

2 Use rounding to estimate the sum of 991 and 2,176. Then find the exact sum.

3 Use rounding to estimate the sum of 6,676 and 2,855. Then find the exact sum.

TAKING ON THE B.E.S.T.

What is subtraction?

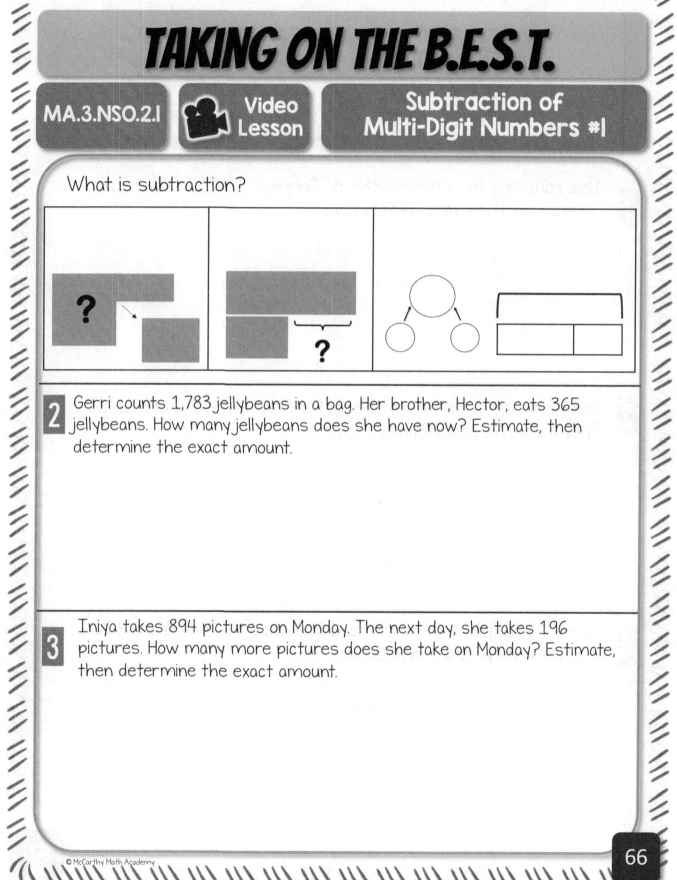

2 Gerri counts 1,783 jellybeans in a bag. Her brother, Hector, eats 365 jellybeans. How many jellybeans does she have now? Estimate, then determine the exact amount.

3 Iniya takes 894 pictures on Monday. The next day, she takes 196 pictures. How many more pictures does she take on Monday? Estimate, then determine the exact amount.

© McCarthy Math Academy

TAKING ON THE B.E.S.T.

1 Use rounding to estimate the difference of 135 from 918. Then, find the exact difference.

2 Use rounding to estimate the difference of 858 from 1,002. Then find the exact difference.

3 Use rounding to estimate the difference of 344 from 8,784. Then find the exact difference.

TAKING ON THE B.E.S.T.

 Video Lesson

Subtraction of Multi-Digit Numbers #2

What is subtraction?

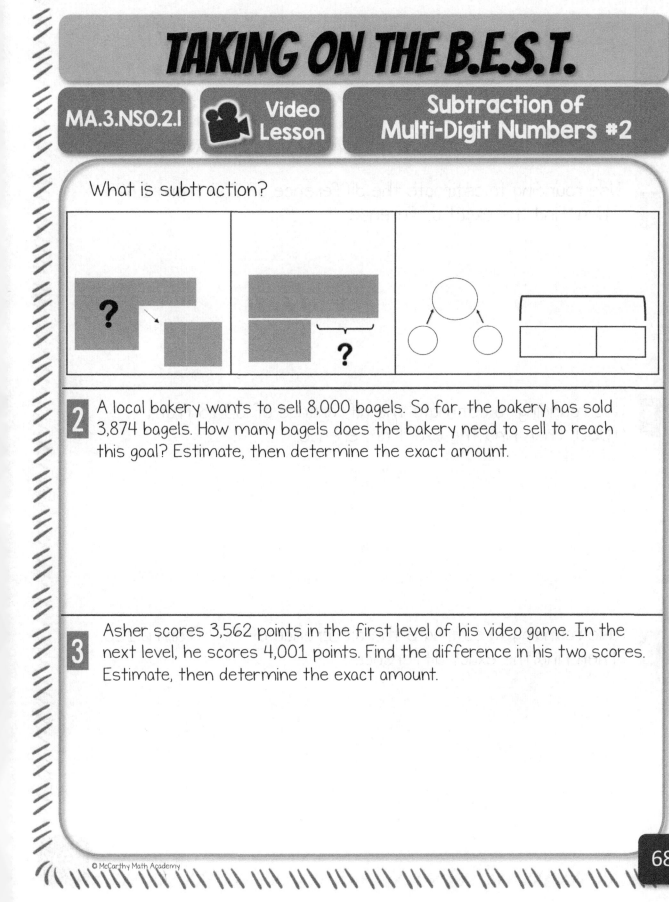

2 A local bakery wants to sell 8,000 bagels. So far, the bakery has sold 3,874 bagels. How many bagels does the bakery need to sell to reach this goal? Estimate, then determine the exact amount.

3 Asher scores 3,562 points in the first level of his video game. In the next level, he scores 4,001 points. Find the difference in his two scores. Estimate, then determine the exact amount.

© McCarthy Math Academy

TAKING ON THE B.E.S.T.

1 Use rounding to estimate the difference of 753 from 1,825. Then, find the exact difference.

2 Use rounding to estimate the difference of 8,118 from 9,000. Then find the exact difference.

3 Use rounding to estimate the difference of 569 from 6,120. Then find the exact difference.

| MA.3.NSO.2.1 | Extra Practice #5 | Word Problems: Addition and Subtraction #1 |

1 Peter creates a goal to read 800 pages this month. If he has read 487 pages, how many more pages must he read to meet his goal?

2 Wendy travels 469 miles to get to her grandmother's house for a family reunion. Then, she drives the same distance back. How many miles does she drive in all?

3 Sandy Palm Elementary has 1,819 students. There are 324 enrolled in third grade. How many students are not enrolled in 3rd grade?

| MA.3.NSO.2.1 | Extra Practice #6 | Word Problems: Addition and Subtraction #2 |

1 Peter reads 800 pages last month. This month, he reads 487 pages. How many pages has he read in the two months combined?

2 Wendy travels 469 miles to her grandmother's house for a family reunion. Her brother, John, travels 272 miles to his grandmother's house for the same reunion. How much farther did Wendy travel?

3 Sandy Palm Elementary has 1,819 students. There are 324 students enrolled in Mossy Oak Elementary. How many students are enrolled in the two schools combined?

TAKING ON THE B.E.S.T.

Tyshanti tracks her running for the month.

She records her running times in the chart to the right.

Tyshanti's Running Tracker For August (in Minutes)	
Week 1	119 minutes
Week 2	163 minutes
Week 3	87 minutes
Week 4	77 minutes

PART ONE

Create an addition word problem using Tyshanti's chart.

_____

_____

_____

Then, solve your word problem.

PART TWO

Create a subtraction word problem using Tyshanti's chart.

_____

_____

_____

Then, solve your word problem.

© McCarthy Math Academy

TAKING ON THE B.E.S.T.

Math Misconception Mystery #1
(PAGE 1)

BEFORE THE VIDEO: Solve the problem on your own.

Find the sum of 4,199 and 3,873.

DURING THE VIDEO: Pause after each "character" solves the problem and jot down quick notes to help you remember what they did correctly or incorrectly.

Character #1 _____

Character #2 _____

Character #3 _____

Character #4 _____

© McCarthy Math Academy

73

TAKING ON THE B.E.S.T.

MA.3.NSO.2.1 | Math Misconception Mystery #1 (PAGE 2)

AFTER THE VIDEO: Discuss and analyze their answers.

The most reasonable answer belongs to Character # _____ because

_____

_____

_____

_____

(Justify how this character's work makes sense.)

Let's help the others:

	Character #___:	Character #___:	Character #___:
What did this character do that was correct?			
Identify their error			
What do they need to know to understand for next time?			

© McCarthy Math Academy

TAKING ON THE B.E.S.T.

Math Misconception Mystery #2
(PAGE I)

BEFORE THE VIDEO: Solve the problem on your own.

Find the difference of 9,000 and 845.

DURING THE VIDEO: Pause after each "character" solves the problem and jot down quick notes to help you remember what they did correctly or incorrectly. .

Character #1 _____

Character #2 _____

Character #3 _____

Character #4 _____

© McCarthy Math Academy

TAKING ON THE B.E.S.T.

Math Misconception Mystery #2 (PAGE 2)

AFTER THE VIDEO: Discuss and analyze their answers.

The most reasonable answer belongs to Character # _____ because

_____

_____

_____

_____

(Justify how this character's work makes sense.)

Let's help the others:

	Character #___:	Character #___:	Character #___:
What did this character do that was correct?			
Identify their error			
What do they need to know to understand for next time?			

© McCarthy Math Academy

TAKING ON THE B.E.S.T.

  Video Lesson | **What is Multiplication?**

1 Ms. McCarthy has 3 paper bags. She places 4 apples in each bag. How many apples are there altogether?

MANIPULATIVES	DRAWING	EQUATION(S)

2 Ms. McCarthy organizes desks into 3 rows with 5 desks in each row. How many desks are there in all?

MANIPULATIVES	DRAWING	EQUATION(S)

TAKING ON THE B.E.S.T.

| MA.3.NSO.2.2 | Extra Practice #1 | What is Multiplication? |

1 Every day, for 3 days, James reads 10 pages of his book. How many pages has he read in all?

MANIPULATIVES	DRAWING	EQUATION(S)

2 Ms. McCarthy organizes desks into 4 rows with 6 desks in each row. How many desks are there in all?

MANIPULATIVES	DRAWING	EQUATION(S)

© McCarthy Math Academy

TAKING ON THE B.E.S.T.

  **Video Lesson** **Multiplication Strategies**

Find the product of 2 and 7.

1

GROUPS OF EQUAL THINGS	ARRAY	EQUATION(S)

Find the product of 4 and 4.

2

GROUPS OF EQUAL THINGS	ARRAY	EQUATION(S)

Find the product of 8 and 3.

3

GROUPS OF EQUAL THINGS	ARRAY	EQUATION(S)

TAKING ON THE B.E.S.T.

1 Find the product of 5 and 4.

GROUPS OF EQUAL THINGS	ARRAY	EQUATION(S)

2 Find the product of 9 and 1.

GROUPS OF EQUAL THINGS	ARRAY	EQUATION(S)

3 Find the product of 2 and 11.

GROUPS OF EQUAL THINGS	ARRAY	EQUATION(S)

TAKING ON THE B.E.S.T.

MA.3.NSO.2.2 **Extra Practice #3** **Multiplication Strategies**

1 Find the product of 1 and 12.

GROUPS OF EQUAL THINGS	ARRAY	EQUATION(S)

2 Find the product of 8 and 4.

GROUPS OF EQUAL THINGS	ARRAY	EQUATION(S)

3 Find the product of 3 and 3.

GROUPS OF EQUAL THINGS	ARRAY	EQUATION(S)

© McCarthy Math Academy

TAKING ON THE B.E.S.T.

1 Find the product of 2 and 12.

GROUPS OF EQUAL THINGS	ARRAY	EQUATION(S)

2 Find the product of 4 and 7.

GROUPS OF EQUAL THINGS	ARRAY	EQUATION(S)

3 Find the product of 7 and 7.

GROUPS OF EQUAL THINGS	ARRAY	EQUATION(S)

© McCarthy Math Academy

TAKING ON THE B.E.S.T.

  **What is Division?**

1 Ms. McCarthy has 12 apples. She places them equally into 3 bags. How many apples are in each bag?

MANIPULATIVES	DRAWING	EQUATION(S)

2 Ms. McCarthy has 15 desks. She creates rows of 5 desks. How many rows of desks does she create?

MANIPULATIVES	DRAWING	EQUATION(S)

© McCarthy Math Academy

1 Hannah has 18 coins. She places them into 2 equal stacks. How many coins are in each stack?

MANIPULATIVES	DRAWING	EQUATION(S)

2 Eduardo has 35 beads. He needs 7 beads to make a bracelet. How many bracelets can he make?

MANIPULATIVES	DRAWING	EQUATION(S)

© McCarthy Math Academy

TAKING ON THE B.E.S.T.

  Video Lesson | **Division Strategies**

Find the quotient of 21 and 7.

1

Divisor is the Number of Groups	Divisor is the Number in Each Group	Equation(s)

2 Find the quotient of 24 and 2.

Divisor is the Number of Groups	Divisor is the Number in Each Group	Equation(s)

3 Find the quotient of 36 and 6.

Divisor is the Number of Groups	Divisor is the Number in Each Group	Equation(s)

© McCarthy Math Academy

TAKING ON THE B.E.S.T.

1. Find the quotient of 18 and 6.

Divisor is the Number of Groups	Divisor is the Number in Each Group	Equation(s)

2. Find the quotient of 10 and 5.

Divisor is the Number of Groups	Divisor is the Number in Each Group	Equation(s)

3. Find the quotient of 4 and 1.

Divisor is the Number of Groups	Divisor is the Number in Each Group	Equation(s)

TAKING ON THE B.E.S.T.

Extra Practice #7

Division Strategies

1 Find the quotient of 7 and 1.

Divisor is the Number of Groups	Divisor is the Number in Each Group	Equation(s)

2 Find the quotient of 16 and 8.

Divisor is the Number of Groups	Divisor is the Number in Each Group	Equation(s)

3 Find the quotient of 49 and 7.

Divisor is the Number of Groups	Divisor is the Number in Each Group	Equation(s)

© McCarthy Math Academy

TAKING ON THE B.E.S.T.

Find the quotient of 14 and 2.

1

Divisor is the Number of Groups	Divisor is the Number in Each Group	Equation(s)

Find the quotient of 40 and 4.

2

Divisor is the Number of Groups	Divisor is the Number in Each Group	Equation(s)

Find the quotient of 64 and 8.

3

Divisor is the Number of Groups	Divisor is the Number in Each Group	Equation(s)

© McCarthy Math Academy

TAKING ON THE B.E.S.T.

  Video Lesson **Multiplication and Division As Inverse Operations**

1 Find the product of 6 and 3.

Model with a Drawing	Write Equation	Fact Family

2 Find the quotient of 32 and 8.

Model with a Drawing	Write Equation	Fact Family

3 Find the product of 8 and 10.

Model with a Drawing	Write Equation	Fact Family

© McCarthy Math Academy

TAKING ON THE B.E.S.T.

1. Find the product of 4 and 5.

Model with a Drawing	Write Equation	Fact Family

2. Find the quotient of 12 and 3.

Model with a Drawing	Write Equation	Fact Family

3. Find the product of 6 and 10.

Model with a Drawing	Write Equation	Fact Family

TAKING ON THE B.E.S.T.

1 Find the product of 8 and 5.

Model with a Drawing	Write Equation	Fact Family

2 Find the quotient of 36 and 3.

Model with a Drawing	Write Equation	Fact Family

3 Find the product of 7 and 11.

Model with a Drawing	Write Equation	Fact Family

© McCarthy Math Academy

TAKING ON THE B.E.S.T.

MA.3.NSO.2.2	Math Mission	Explore Multiplication and Division

PART ONE

Use the numbers to create a **multiplication equation** and a **division equation**: 32, 8, 4

☐ X ☐ = ☐   ☐ ÷ ☐ = ☐

PART TWO:

Create a word problem based on the multiplication equation.

_____

_____

_____

_____

Then, solve your word problem.

PART THREE:

Rewrite your word problem to describe your division equation.

_____

_____

_____

Then, solve your word problem.

© McCarthy Math Academy

TAKING ON THE B.E.S.T.

Math Misconception Mystery #1 (PAGE 1)

BEFORE THE VIDEO: Solve the problem on your own.

Find the product of 12 and 6.

DURING THE VIDEO: Pause after each "character" solves the problem and jot down quick notes to help you remember what they did correctly or incorrectly.

Character #1 _____

Character #2 _____

Character #3 _____

Character #4 _____

© McCarthy Math Academy

TAKING ON THE B.E.S.T.

Math Misconception Mystery #1 (PAGE 2)

AFTER THE VIDEO: Discuss and analyze their answers.

The most reasonable answer belongs to Character # _____ because

_____

_____

_____

_____

(Justify how this character's work makes sense.)

Let's help the others:

	Character #___:	Character #___:	Character #___:
What did this character do that was correct?			
Identify their error			
What do they need to know to understand for next time?			

© McCarthy Math Academy

TAKING ON THE B.E.S.T.

MA.3.NSO.2.2 | Math Misconception Mystery #2 (PAGE 1)

BEFORE THE VIDEO: Solve the problem on your own.

> Find the quotient of 8 and 4.

DURING THE VIDEO: Pause after each "character" solves the problem and jot down quick notes to help you remember what they did correctly or incorrectly.

Character #1 _____	Character #2 _____
Character #3 _____	**Character #4** _____

TAKING ON THE B.E.S.T.

Math Misconception Mystery #2
(PAGE 2)

AFTER THE VIDEO: Discuss and analyze their answers.

The most reasonable answer belongs to Character # _____ because

_____

_____

_____

_____

(Justify how this character's work makes sense.)

Let's help the others:

	Character #___:	Character #___:	Character #___:
What did this character do that was correct?			
Identify their error			
What do they need to know to understand for next time?			

© McCarthy Math Academy

MA.3.NSO.2.3  **Video Lesson** **Multiply a 1-Digit Whole Number by a Multiple of 10**

Find the product of 3 x 20.

1

MANIPULATIVES	DRAWING	EQUATION(S)

2 Find the product of 50 x 4.

MANIPULATIVES	DRAWING	EQUATION(S)

© McCarthy Math Academy

TAKING ON THE B.E.S.T.

| MA.3.NSO.2.3 | Extra Practice #1 | Multiply a 1-Digit Whole Number by a Multiple of 10 |

Find the product of 8 x 30.

1

MANIPULATIVES	DRAWING	EQUATION(S)

2 **Find the product of 40 x 1.**

MANIPULATIVES	DRAWING	EQUATION(S)

© McCarthy Math Academy

TAKING ON THE B.E.S.T.

MA.3.NSO.2.3 | **Extra Practice #2** | **Multiply a 1-Digit Whole Number by a Multiple of 10**

1 Find the product of 5 x 90.

MANIPULATIVES	DRAWING	EQUATION(S)

2 Find the product of 80 x 4.

MANIPULATIVES	DRAWING	EQUATION(S)

TAKING ON THE B.E.S.T.

  Video Lesson | **Multiply a 1-Digit Whole Number by a Multiple of 100**

1 Find the product of 4 x 600.

MANIPULATIVES	DRAWING	EQUATION(S)

2 Find the product of 700 x 6.

MANIPULATIVES	DRAWING	EQUATION(S)

© McCarthy Math Academy

TAKING ON THE B.E.S.T.

1 Find the product of 2 x 200.

MANIPULATIVES	DRAWING	EQUATION(S)

2 Find the product of 300 x 6.

MANIPULATIVES	DRAWING	EQUATION(S)

1 Find the product of 6 x 800.

MANIPULATIVES	DRAWING	EQUATION(S)

2 Find the product of 100 x 8.

MANIPULATIVES	DRAWING	EQUATION(S)

© McCarthy Math Academy

TAKING ON THE B.E.S.T.

| MA.3.NSO.2.3 | Math Mission | Multiply a 1-Digit Whole Number by a Multiple of 10 or 100 |

The local science center has the following list of purchase options.

PART ONE

The Suarez family wants to purchase day passes to the local science center. They will need 3 adult passes and 2 child passes. How much should they expect to spend for the day?

TICKET	COST
Adult - One Day	$60
Child - One Day	$40
Adult - Annual Pass	$500
Child - Annual Pass	$300

Explain how you know using words, a picture, or equations.

PART TWO

The Galasso family wants to buy 2 adult annual passes, 4 child annual passes, and 4 adult day passes. How much should they expect to spend?

Explain how you know using words, a picture, or equations.

TAKING ON THE B.E.S.T.

Math Misconception Mystery
(PAGE 1)

BEFORE THE VIDEO: Solve the problem on your own.

Find the product of 6 and 500.

DURING THE VIDEO: Pause after each "character" solves the problem and jot down quick notes to help you remember what they did correctly or incorrectly.

Character #1 _____

Character #2 _____

Character #3 _____

Character #4 _____

© McCarthy Math Academy

TAKING ON THE B.E.S.T.

Math Misconception Mystery
(PAGE 2)

AFTER THE VIDEO: Discuss and analyze their answers.

The most reasonable answer belongs to Character # _____ because

_____

_____

_____

_____

(Justify how this character's work makes sense.)

Let's help the others:

	Character #___:	Character #___:	Character #___:
What did this character do that was correct?			
Identify their error			
What do they need to know to understand for next time?			

TAKING ON THE B.E.S.T.

  Video Lesson | The Commutative Property of Multiplication

1 Find the product of 7 and 3.

ORIGINAL MODEL	COMMUTATIVE PROPERTY OF MULTIPLICATION MODEL	RELATED FACTS

2 Find the product of 4 and 9.

ORIGINAL MODEL	COMMUTATIVE PROPERTY OF MULTIPLICATION MODEL	RELATED FACTS

© McCarthy Math Academy

TAKING ON THE B.E.S.T.

Extra Practice #1 | **The Commutative Property of Multiplication**

1 Find the product of 6 and 4.

ORIGINAL MODEL	COMMUTATIVE PROPERTY OF MULTIPLICATION MODEL	RELATED FACTS

2 Find the product of 3 and 5.

ORIGINAL MODEL	COMMUTATIVE PROPERTY OF MULTIPLICATION MODEL	RELATED FACTS

© McCarthy Math Academy

TAKING ON THE B.E.S.T.

1 Find the product of 10 and 3.

ORIGINAL MODEL	COMMUTATIVE PROPERTY OF MULTIPLICATION MODEL	RELATED FACTS

2 Find the product of 6 and 3.

ORIGINAL MODEL	COMMUTATIVE PROPERTY OF MULTIPLICATION MODEL	RELATED FACTS

© McCarthy Math Academy

TAKING ON THE B.E.S.T.

  Video Lesson | **The Associative Property of Multiplication**

1 Find the product of 2 x 3 x 4.

METHOD #1	METHOD #2	CONNECT IT TO THE REAL WORD

2 Find the product of 3 x 5 x 4.

METHOD #1	METHOD #2	CONNECT IT TO THE REAL WORD

© McCarthy Math Academy

TAKING ON THE B.E.S.T.

1 Find the product of 2 x 3 x 2.

METHOD #1	METHOD #2	CONNECT IT TO THE REAL WORD

2 Find the product of 2 x 10 x 5.

METHOD #1	METHOD #2	CONNECT IT TO THE REAL WORD

TAKING ON THE B.E.S.T.

MA.3.NSO.2.4 | **Extra Practice #4** | **The Associative Property of Multiplication**

---

1 Find the product of 1 x 6 x 4.

METHOD #1	METHOD #2	CONNECT IT TO THE REAL WORD

---

2 Find the product of 5 x 2 x 6.

METHOD #1	METHOD #2	CONNECT IT TO THE REAL WORD

© McCarthy Math Academy

TAKING ON THE B.E.S.T.

  Video Lesson | The Distributive Property of Multiplication

1 Find the product of 6 x 11.

METHOD #1	METHOD #2	EXPLAIN ONE METHOD IN WORDS

2 Find the product of 8 x 7.

METHOD #1	METHOD #2	EXPLAIN ONE METHOD IN WORDS

© McCarthy Math Academy

TAKING ON THE B.E.S.T.

MA.3.NSO.2.4 · **Extra Practice #5** · **The Distributive Property of Multiplication**

1 Find the product of 12 x 11.

METHOD #1	METHOD #2	EXPLAIN ONE METHOD IN WORDS

2 Find the product of 6 x 8.

METHOD #1	METHOD #2	EXPLAIN ONE METHOD IN WORDS

© McCarthy Math Academy

TAKING ON THE B.E.S.T.

1 Find the product of 11 x 11.

METHOD #1	METHOD #2	EXPLAIN ONE METHOD IN WORDS

2 Find the product of 9 x 12.

METHOD #1	METHOD #2	EXPLAIN ONE METHOD IN WORDS

© McCarthy Math Academy

TAKING ON THE B.E.S.T.

| MA.3.NSO.2.4 | Math Mission | Properties of Multiplication |

PART ONE

Auggie is trying to model the Commutative Property of Multiplication. Analyze his work below and describe his error.

$4 \times 2 = 8$ $2 \times 4 = 8$

PART TWO

Auggie wants to use the Distributive Property of Multiplication to solve 6 x 9. He has already drawn the array with a line to break apart one factor. Now, Auggie is stuck and not sure what the next step is.

How would you guide Auggie using the Distributive Property of Multiplication?

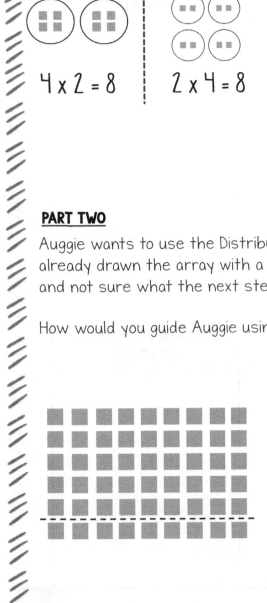

TAKING ON THE B.E.S.T.

Math Misconception Mystery
(PAGE 1)

BEFORE THE VIDEO: Solve the problem on your own.

Which of the following does NOT have the same value has 11×4?

Ⓐ 4×11

Ⓑ $(2 \times 2) \times 11$

Ⓒ $(10 \times 4) + (1 \times 4)$

Ⓓ $(10 + 4) + (1 + 4)$

DURING THE VIDEO: Pause after each "character" solves the problem and jot down quick notes to help you remember what they did correctly or incorrectly.

Character #1 _____

Character #2 _____

Character #3 _____

Character #4 _____

TAKING ON THE B.E.S.T.

Math Misconception Mystery (PAGE 2)

AFTER THE VIDEO: Discuss and analyze their answers.

The most reasonable answer belongs to Character # _____ because

_____

_____

_____

_____

(Justify how this character's work makes sense.)

Let's help the others:

	Character #___:	Character #___:	Character #___:
What did this character do that was correct?			
Identify their error			
What do they need to know to understand for next time?			

TAKING ON THE B.E.S.T.

  Video Lesson | **Representing Unit Fractions (Area Model)**

Represent each unit fraction by creating an area model.

1

$$\frac{1}{2}$$

2

$$\frac{1}{5}$$

3

$$\frac{1}{10}$$

© McCarthy Math Academy

TAKING ON THE B.E.S.T.

Represent each unit fraction by creating an area model.

1

$$\frac{1}{3}$$

2

$$\frac{1}{8}$$

3

$$\frac{1}{12}$$

© McCarthy Math Academy

TAKING ON THE B.E.S.T.

 Video Lesson

Representing Unit Fractions (On a Number Line)

Represent each unit fraction on a number line.

1

$\frac{1}{2}$

2

$\frac{1}{4}$

3

$\frac{1}{10}$

© McCarthy Math Academy

TAKING ON THE B.E.S.T.

Extra Practice #2

Representing Unit Fractions (On a Number Line)

Represent each unit fraction on a number line.

1

$\dfrac{1}{3}$

2

$\dfrac{1}{8}$

3

$\dfrac{1}{12}$

© McCarthy Math Academy

TAKING ON THE B.E.S.T.

Represent each unit fraction as a set.

1

$$\frac{1}{2}$$

2

$$\frac{1}{4}$$

3

$$\frac{1}{10}$$

122

TAKING ON THE B.E.S.T.

Represent each unit fraction as a set.

1 $\dfrac{1}{3}$

2 $\dfrac{1}{8}$

3 $\dfrac{1}{12}$

© McCarthy Math Academy

TAKING ON THE B.E.S.T.

| MA.3.FR.I.I | Math Missions | Representing Unit Fractions |

You are given the unit fraction $\frac{1}{5}$.

PART ONE

How can you represent this fraction as an area model in a shape other than a rectangle?

PART TWO

How can you represent this fraction on a number line?

PART THREE

Create a real world scenario to represent this fraction as a set.

_____

_____

_____

_____

© McCarthy Math Academy

TAKING ON THE B.E.S.T.

Math Misconception Mystery (PAGE 1)

BEFORE THE VIDEO: Solve the problem on your own.

Create a model to represent $\frac{1}{12}$.

DURING THE VIDEO: Pause after each "character" solves the problem and jot down quick notes to help you remember what they did correctly or incorrectly.

Character #1 _____	Character #2 _____
Character #3 _____	Character #4 _____

125

© McCarthy Math Academy

TAKING ON THE B.E.S.T.

Math Misconception Mystery
(PAGE 2)

AFTER THE VIDEO: Discuss and analyze their answers.

The most reasonable answer belongs to Character # _____ because

_____

_____

_____

_____

(Justify how this character's work makes sense.)

Let's help the others:

	Character #___:	Character #___:	Character #___:
What did this character do that was correct?			
Identify their error			
What do they need to know to understand for next time?			

126

TAKING ON THE B.E.S.T.

 Video Lesson

Represent Fractions as a Sum of Unit Fractions #1

Represent each fraction as a sum of unit fractions. Include an area model and model on a number line.

1 $\dfrac{3}{8}$

2 $\dfrac{5}{5}$

3 $\dfrac{6}{10}$

© McCarthy Math Academy

TAKING ON THE B.E.S.T.

Represent each fraction as a sum of unit fractions. Include an area model and model on a number line.

1 $\dfrac{5}{6}$

2 $\dfrac{7}{12}$

3 $\dfrac{4}{4}$

© McCarthy Math Academy

TAKING ON THE B.E.S.T.

Represent each fraction as a sum of unit fractions. Include an area model and model on a number line.

1 $\dfrac{10}{5}$

2 $\dfrac{7}{3}$

3 $\dfrac{5}{2}$

© McCarthy Math Academy

TAKING ON THE B.E.S.T.

Represent each fraction as a sum of unit fractions. Include an area model and model on a number line.

1 $\dfrac{11}{8}$

2 $\dfrac{8}{4}$

3 $\dfrac{9}{2}$

© McCarthy Math Academy

TAKING ON THE B.E.S.T.

MA.3.FR.I.2 | Math Missions | Representing Unit Fractions

PART ONE

How many one—sixth pieces would you need to create one whole? Prove your thinking using an area model and a number line.

PART TWO

How many one—sixth pieces would you need to create three wholes? Prove your thinking using an area model and a number line.

PART THREE

Write $\frac{11}{6}$ as a sum of unit fractions.

© McCarthy Math Academy

TAKING ON THE B.E.S.T.

Math Misconception Mystery
(PAGE 1)

BEFORE THE VIDEO: Solve the problem on your own.

Which of the following expressions represents $\frac{4}{3}$?

Ⓐ $\frac{1}{3} + \frac{1}{3} + \frac{1}{3}$

Ⓑ $\frac{1}{4} + \frac{1}{4} + \frac{1}{4}$

Ⓒ $\frac{1}{3} + \frac{1}{3} + \frac{1}{3} + \frac{1}{3}$

Ⓓ $\frac{1}{4} + \frac{1}{4} + \frac{1}{4} + \frac{1}{4}$

DURING THE VIDEO: Pause after each "character" solves the problem and jot down quick notes to help you remember what they did correctly or incorrectly.

Character #1 _____	Character #2 _____
Character #3 _____	Character #4 _____

132

© McCarthy Math Academy

TAKING ON THE B.E.S.T.

MA.3.FR.1.2

Math Misconception Mystery
(PAGE 2)

AFTER THE VIDEO: Discuss and analyze their answers.

The most reasonable answer belongs to Character # _____ because

_____

_____

_____

_____

(Justify how this character's work makes sense.)

Let's help the others:

	Character #___:	Character #___:	Character #___:
What did this character do that was correct?			
Identify their error			
What do they need to know to understand for next time?			

133

© McCarthy Math Academy

TAKING ON THE B.E.S.T.

MA.3.FR.I.3  **Video Lesson** | **Read and Write Fractions Less Than Or Equal to One**

Represent each fraction in standard form, numeral–word form, and word form.

1

STANDARD FORM	NUMERAL-WORD FORM	WORD FORM
$\frac{2}{6}$		

2

STANDARD FORM	NUMERAL-WORD FORM	WORD FORM
	7 tenths	

3

STANDARD FORM	NUMERAL-WORD FORM	WORD FORM
		eleven twelfths

© McCarthy Math Academy

TAKING ON THE B.E.S.T.

| Extra Practice #1 | Read and Write Fractions Less Than Or Equal to One

Represent each fraction in standard form, numeral-word form, and word form.

1

STANDARD FORM	NUMERAL-WORD FORM	WORD FORM
$\dfrac{3}{5}$		

2

STANDARD FORM	NUMERAL-WORD FORM	WORD FORM
	4 eighths	

3

STANDARD FORM	NUMERAL-WORD FORM	WORD FORM
		two thirds

135

© McCarthy Math Academy

TAKING ON THE B.E.S.T.

Represent each fraction in standard form, numeral–word form, word form, and as a mixed number.

1

STANDARD FORM	NUMERAL-WORD FORM	WORD FORM	MIXED NUMBER
$\dfrac{8}{5}$			

2

STANDARD FORM	NUMERAL-WORD FORM	WORD FORM	MIXED NUMBER
	4 thirds		

3

STANDARD FORM	NUMERAL-WORD FORM	WORD FORM	MIXED NUMBER
		Five halves	

136

© McCarthy Math Academy

TAKING ON THE B.E.S.T.

Represent each fraction in standard form, numeral–word form, word form, and as a mixed number.

1

STANDARD FORM	NUMERAL-WORD FORM	WORD FORM	MIXED NUMBER
$\dfrac{6}{4}$			

2

STANDARD FORM	NUMERAL-WORD FORM	WORD FORM	MIXED NUMBER
	10 sixths		

3

STANDARD FORM	NUMERAL-WORD FORM	WORD FORM	MIXED NUMBER
		twenty-three tenths	

TAKING ON THE B.E.S.T.

MA.3.FR.1.3	Math Missions	Read and Write Fractions

Mr. Mulch is in the middle of painting a room. The model below represents how much of the room he has painted.

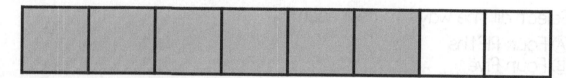

PART ONE

Write the fraction of the room he has completed painting in standard form.

PART TWO

Write the fraction of the room he has completed painting in numeral–word form.

PART THREE

Write the fraction of the room he has completed painting in word form.

© McCarthy Math Academy

TAKING ON THE B.E.S.T.

MA.3.FR.I.3 | Math Misconception Mystery (PAGE I)

BEFORE THE VIDEO: Solve the problem on your own.

Select all the ways to represent $\frac{5}{4}$.

Ⓐ Four fifths
Ⓑ Four five
Ⓒ Five fourths
Ⓓ Five fours
Ⓔ Five and one fourth
Ⓕ One and one fourth

DURING THE VIDEO: Pause after each "character" solves the problem and jot down quick notes to help you remember what they did correctly or incorrectly.

Character #1 _____

Character #2 _____

Character #3 _____

Character #4 _____

139

© McCarthy Math Academy

TAKING ON THE B.E.S.T.

Math Misconception Mystery (PAGE 2)

AFTER THE VIDEO: Discuss and analyze their answers.

The most reasonable answer belongs to Character # _____ because
_____
_____
_____
_____

(Justify how this character's work makes sense.)

Let's help the others:

	Character #___:	Character #___:	Character #___:
What did this character do that was correct?			
Identify their error			
What do they need to know to understand for next time?			

140

© McCarthy Math Academy

TAKING ON THE B.E.S.T.

MA.3.FR.2.1 | 🎥 **Video Lesson** | **Comparing Two Fractions Using a Number Line**

1 Compare $\frac{2}{4}$ and $\frac{2}{3}$ using the number lines.

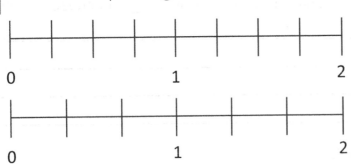

0   1   2

0   1   2

Use <, >, or = to compare the fractions.

$\frac{2}{4}$ ◯ $\frac{2}{3}$

---

2 Compare $\frac{4}{5}$ and $\frac{3}{5}$ using the number lines.

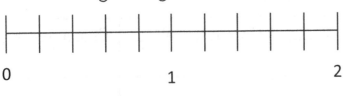

0   1   2

0   1   2

Use <, >, or = to compare the fractions.

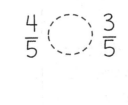

$\frac{4}{5}$ ◯ $\frac{3}{5}$

---

3 Compare $\frac{6}{6}$ and $\frac{6}{8}$ using the number lines.

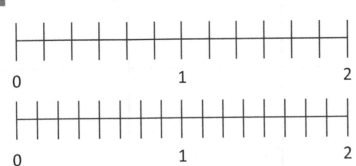

0   1   2

0   1   2

Use <, >, or = to compare the fractions.

$\frac{6}{6}$ ◯ $\frac{6}{8}$

© McCarthy Math Academy

TAKING ON THE B.E.S.T.

MA.3.FR.2.1	Extra Practice #1	Comparing Two Fractions Using a Number Line

1 Compare $\frac{3}{4}$ and $\frac{3}{3}$ using the number lines.

Use <, >, or = to compare the fractions.

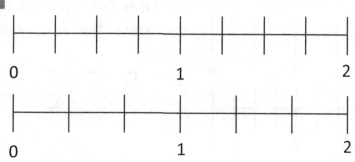

$$\frac{3}{4} \bigcirc \frac{3}{3}$$

2 Compare $\frac{2}{6}$ and $\frac{5}{6}$ using the number lines.

Use <, >, or = to compare the fractions.

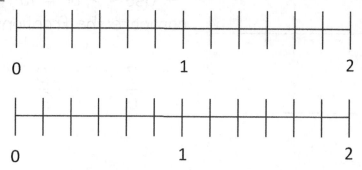

$$\frac{2}{6} \bigcirc \frac{5}{6}$$

3 1. Compare $\frac{2}{4}$ and $\frac{2}{8}$ using the number lines.

Use <, >, or = to compare the fractions.

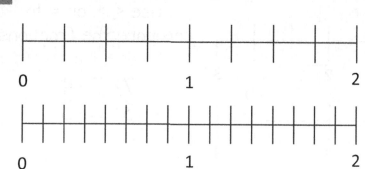

$$\frac{2}{4} \bigcirc \frac{2}{8}$$

© McCarthy Math Academy

TAKING ON THE B.E.S.T.

1 Compare $\frac{5}{2}$ and $\frac{5}{4}$ using the number lines.

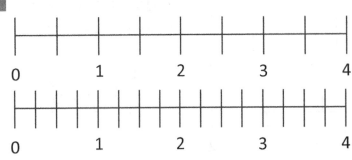

Use <, >, or = to compare the fractions.

$$\frac{5}{2} \bigcirc \frac{5}{4}$$

---

2 Compare $\frac{7}{6}$ and $\frac{10}{6}$ using the number lines.

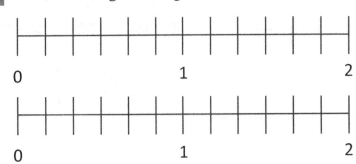

Use <, >, or = to compare the fractions.

$$\frac{7}{6} \bigcirc \frac{10}{6}$$

---

3 Compare $\frac{7}{3}$ and $\frac{4}{3}$ using the number lines.

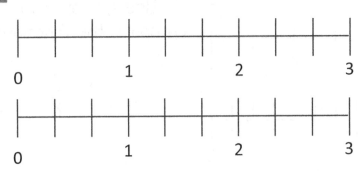

Use <, >, or = to compare the fractions.

$$\frac{7}{3} \bigcirc \frac{4}{3}$$

143

© McCarthy Math Academy

TAKING ON THE B.E.S.T.

1 Compare $\frac{4}{2}$ and $\frac{4}{3}$ using the number lines.

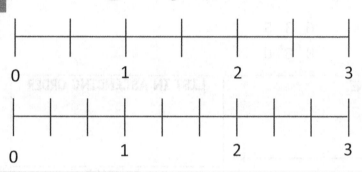

Use <, >, or = to compare the fractions.

$\frac{4}{2}$ ◯ $\frac{4}{3}$

2 Compare $\frac{8}{4}$ and $\frac{4}{4}$ using the number lines.

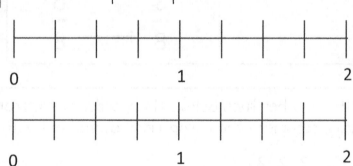

Use <, >, or = to compare the fractions.

$\frac{8}{4}$ ◯ $\frac{4}{4}$

3 Compare $\frac{7}{5}$ and $\frac{7}{6}$ using the number lines.

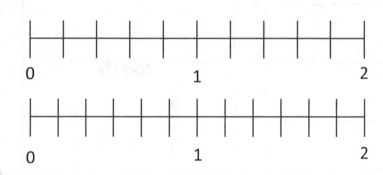

Use <, >, or = to compare the fractions.

$\frac{7}{5}$ ◯ $\frac{7}{6}$

© McCarthy Math Academy

TAKING ON THE B.E.S.T.

 **Video Lesson**

Plot, Order, and Compare Fractions (Number Line)

1 Plot each fraction using the number line below. Then, order them from LEAST to GREATEST. Finally, complete the comparison statement with the correct symbol.

$$\frac{6}{8}, \frac{3}{8}, \frac{5}{8}$$

NUMBER LINE	LIST IN ASCENDING ORDER
0 ———————————————— 1	
	COMPARE
	$\frac{3}{8}$ —— $\frac{6}{8}$

2 Plot each fraction using the number lines below. Then, order them from LEAST to GREATEST. Finally, complete the comparison statement with the correct symbol.

$$\frac{2}{3}, \frac{2}{4}, \frac{2}{5}$$

NUMBER LINES	LIST IN ASCENDING ORDER
0 ———————————————— 1	
0 ———————————————— 1	
0 ———————————————— 1	**COMPARE**
	$\frac{2}{3}$ —— $\frac{2}{4}$

© McCarthy Math Academy

TAKING ON THE B.E.S.T.

MA3.FR.2.I | **Extra Practice #3** | **Plot, Order, and Compare Fractions (Number Line)**

1 Plot each fraction using the number line below. Then, order them from LEAST to GREATEST. Finally, complete the comparison statement with the correct symbol.

$$\frac{4}{12}, \frac{5}{12}, \frac{9}{12}$$

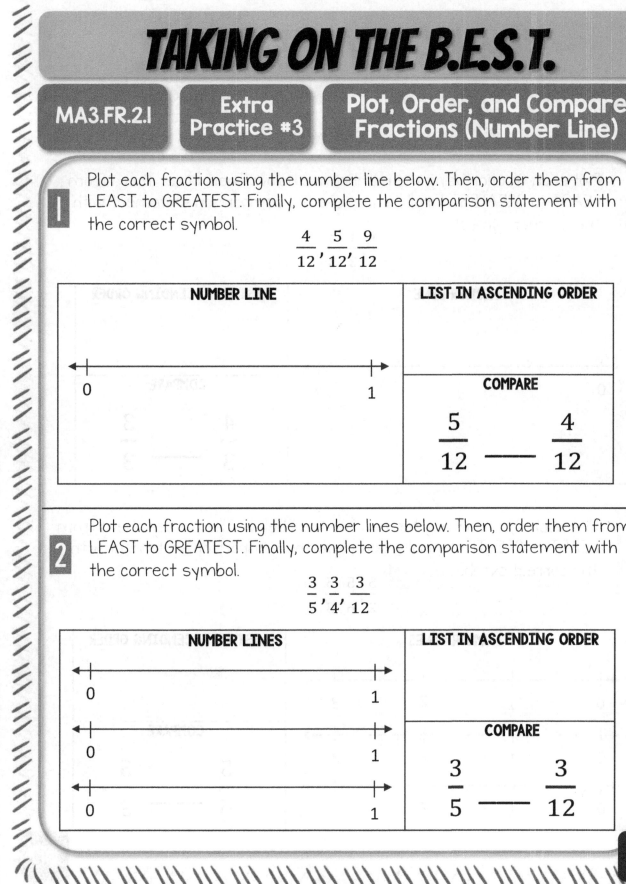

NUMBER LINE

0   1

LIST IN ASCENDING ORDER

COMPARE

$$\frac{5}{12} \rule{1cm}{0.5pt} \frac{4}{12}$$

2 Plot each fraction using the number lines below. Then, order them from LEAST to GREATEST. Finally, complete the comparison statement with the correct symbol.

$$\frac{3}{5}, \frac{3}{4}, \frac{3}{12}$$

NUMBER LINES

0   1

0   1

0   1

LIST IN ASCENDING ORDER

COMPARE

$$\frac{3}{5} \rule{1cm}{0.5pt} \frac{3}{12}$$

146

© McCarthy Math Academy

TAKING ON THE B.E.S.T.

1 Plot each fraction using the number line below. Then, order them from LEAST to GREATEST. Finally, complete the comparison statement with the correct symbol.

$$\frac{4}{3}, \frac{1}{3}, \frac{3}{3}$$

NUMBER LINE	LIST IN ASCENDING ORDER

0   1   2

COMPARE

$$\frac{4}{3} \underline{\hspace{1cm}} \frac{3}{3}$$

2 Plot each fraction using the number lines below. Then, order them from LEAST to GREATEST. Finally, complete the comparison statement with the correct symbol.

$$\frac{5}{2}, \frac{5}{6}, \frac{5}{3}$$

NUMBER LINES	LIST IN ASCENDING ORDER

0   1   2   3

0   1   2   3

0   1   2   3

COMPARE

$$\frac{5}{6} \underline{\hspace{1cm}} \frac{5}{3}$$

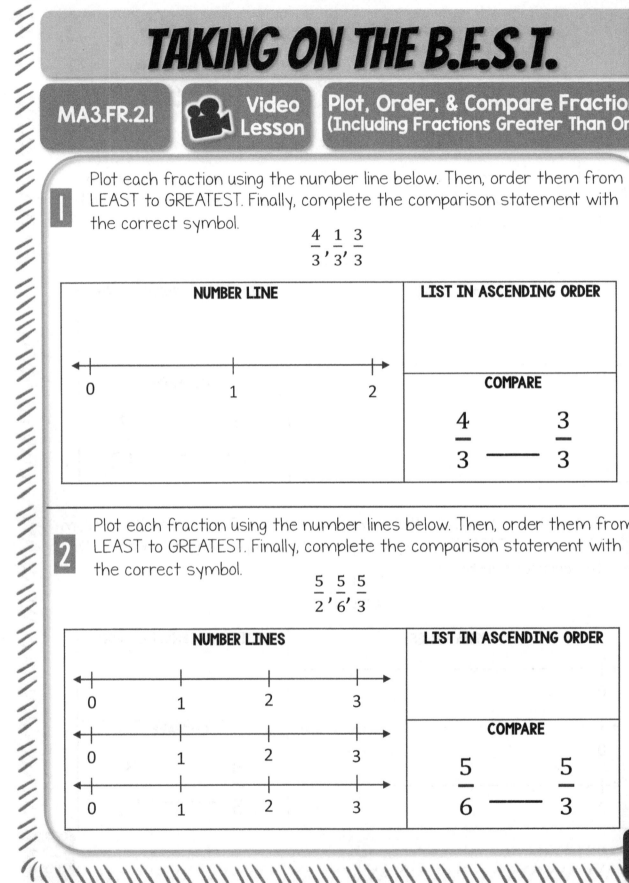

© McCarthy Math Academy

TAKING ON THE B.E.S.T.

MA3.FR.2.I | **Extra Practice #4** | **Plot, Order, & Compare Fractions** (Including Fractions Greater Than One)

1 Plot each fraction using the number line below. Then, order them from LEAST to GREATEST. Finally, complete the comparison statement with the correct symbol.

$$\frac{5}{10}, \frac{17}{10}, \frac{13}{10}$$

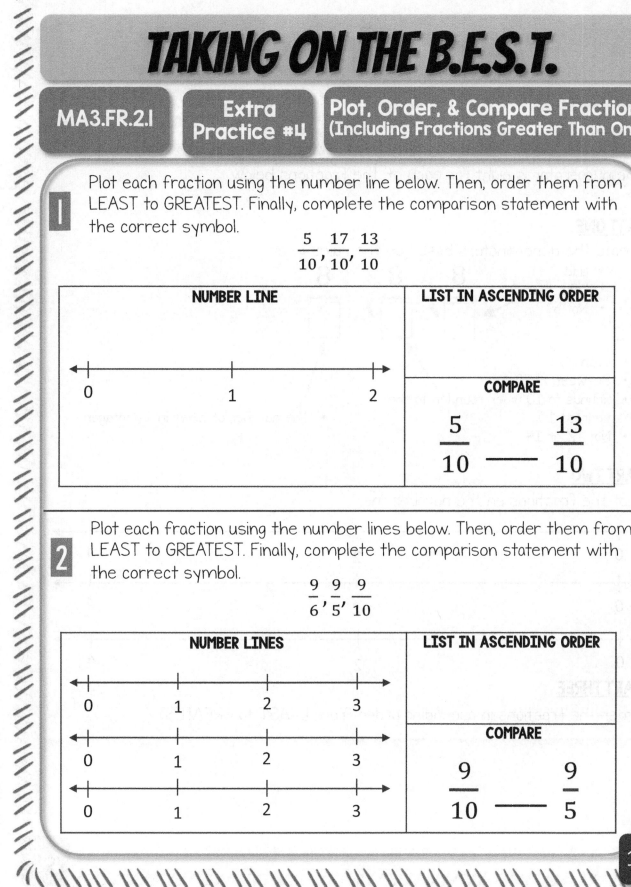

NUMBER LINE	LIST IN ASCENDING ORDER
0 1 2	
	COMPARE
	$\frac{5}{10}$ —— $\frac{13}{10}$

2 Plot each fraction using the number lines below. Then, order them from LEAST to GREATEST. Finally, complete the comparison statement with the correct symbol.

$$\frac{9}{6}, \frac{9}{5}, \frac{9}{10}$$

NUMBER LINES	LIST IN ASCENDING ORDER
0 1 2 3	
0 1 2 3	
0 1 2 3	COMPARE
	$\frac{9}{10}$ —— $\frac{9}{5}$

148

© McCarthy Math Academy

TAKING ON THE B.E.S.T.

MA.3.FR.2.1	Math Missions	Plot, Order and Compare Fractions

The numerator is eight for each of the fractions below.

PART ONE

Create the denominators based on the rules given.

- Odd
- Less than 7
- Not 5

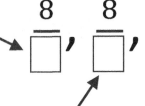

- Even
- Between 2–20,
- Rounds to 10 when rounded to the nearest 10
- Not 12. or 14

- The number of sides in a pentagon

PART TWO

Plot the fractions on the number line.

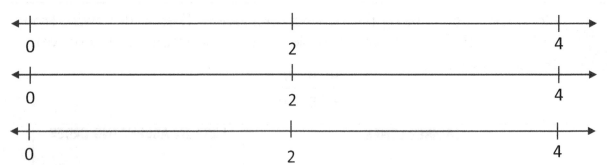

PART THREE

Order the fractions in ascending order from LEAST to GREATEST.

149

© McCarthy Math Academy

TAKING ON THE B.E.S.T.

| MA.3.FR.2.1 | Math Misconception Mystery (PAGE 1) |

BEFORE THE VIDEO: Solve the problem on your own.

> Compare 8 fifths and 9 fifths using <, >, or =.

DURING THE VIDEO: Pause after each "character" solves the problem and jot down quick notes to help you remember what they did correctly or incorrectly.

Character #1 _____	Character #2 _____
Character #3 _____	**Character #4** _____

© McCarthy Math Academy

TAKING ON THE B.E.S.T.

Math Misconception Mystery (PAGE 2)

AFTER THE VIDEO: Discuss and analyze their answers.

The most reasonable answer belongs to Character # _____ because

_____

_____

_____

_____

(Justify how this character's work makes sense.)

Let's help the others:

	Character #___:	Character #___:	Character #___:
What did this character do that was correct?			
Identify their error			
What do they need to know to understand for next time?			

© McCarthy Math Academy

TAKING ON THE B.E.S.T.

1 Determine if $\frac{6}{10}$ and $\frac{3}{5}$ are equivalent by drawing an area model to justify your answer.

_____
_____
_____
_____
_____
_____

2 Determine if $\frac{3}{8}$ and $\frac{2}{4}$ are equivalent by drawing an area model to justify your answer.

_____
_____
_____
_____
_____
_____

3 Determine if $\frac{8}{12}$ and $\frac{4}{6}$ are equivalent by drawing an area model to justify your answer.

_____
_____
_____
_____

152

© McCarthy Math Academy

TAKING ON THE B.E.S.T.

1 Determine if $\frac{2}{3}$ and $\frac{7}{12}$ are equivalent by drawing an area model to justify your answer.

_____
_____
_____
_____
_____

2 Determine if $\frac{1}{2}$ and $\frac{6}{12}$ are equivalent by drawing an area model to justify your answer.

_____
_____
_____
_____
_____

3 Determine if $\frac{3}{4}$ and $\frac{4}{5}$ are equivalent by drawing an area model to justify your answer.

_____
_____
_____
_____

153

© McCarthy Math Academy

1 Determine if $\frac{3}{4}$ and $\frac{6}{8}$ are equivalent using the number lines below.

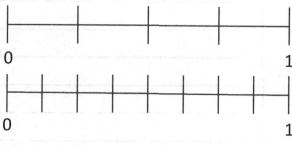

_____
_____
_____
_____
_____

2 Determine if $\frac{1}{6}$ and $\frac{2}{5}$ are equivalent using the number lines below.

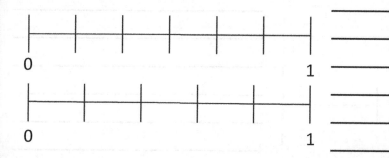

_____
_____
_____
_____
_____

3 Determine if $\frac{2}{6}$ and $\frac{4}{12}$ are equivalent using the number lines below.

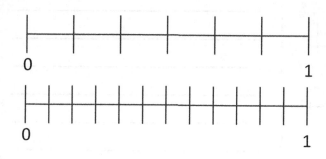

_____
_____
_____
_____
_____

154

© McCarthy Math Academy

TAKING ON THE B.E.S.T.

MA.3.FR.2.2 | **Extra Practice #2** | **Equivalent Fractions (Number Line)**

1 Determine if $\frac{6}{6}$ and $\frac{3}{3}$ are equivalent using the number lines below.

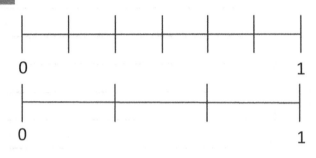

0   1

0   1

_____

_____

_____

_____

2 Determine if $\frac{1}{2}$ and $\frac{1}{3}$ are equivalent using the number lines below.

0   1

0   1

_____

_____

_____

_____

3 Determine if $\frac{3}{8}$ and $\frac{2}{10}$ are equivalent using the number lines below.

0   1

0   1

_____

_____

_____

_____

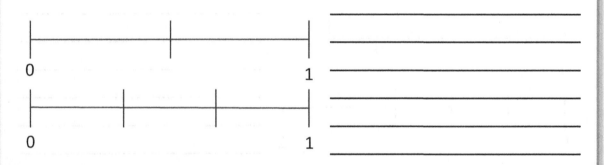

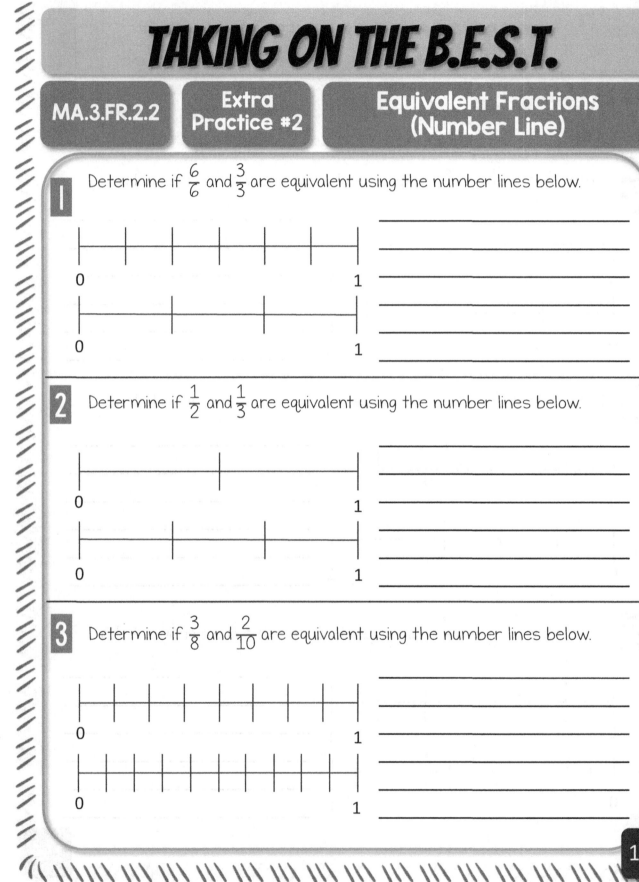

155

© McCarthy Math Academy

TAKING ON THE B.E.S.T.

MA.3.FR.2.2 | **Math Missions** | **Equivalent Fractions**

PART ONE

Use the number lines to determine a fraction with a denominator of eight that is equivalent to $\frac{3}{12}$.

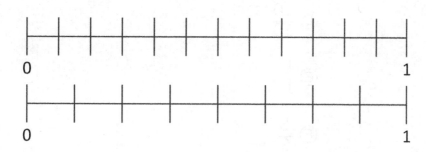

PART TWO

Model the same fractions using area models.

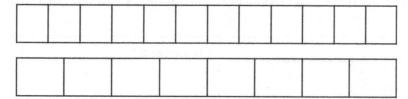

PART THREE

Carson says that 3 eighths is equivalent to 3 twelfths because they both have the same numerator. Explain Carson's error. Use the number lines and area models you have created to justify your reasoning.

_____

_____

_____

_____

© McCarthy Math Academy

TAKING ON THE B.E.S.T.

Math Misconception Mystery
(PAGE I)

BEFORE THE VIDEO: Solve the problem on your own.

Select all the fractions that are equivalent to one whole.

Ⓐ $\frac{4}{3}$

Ⓑ $\frac{2}{2}$

Ⓒ $\frac{7}{8}$

Ⓓ $\frac{10}{10}$

Ⓔ $\frac{1}{1}$

Ⓕ $\frac{5}{6}$

DURING THE VIDEO: Pause after each "character" solves the problem and jot down quick notes to help you remember what they did correctly or incorrectly.

Character #1 _____	Character #2 _____
Character #3 _____	**Character #4** _____

157

TAKING ON THE B.E.S.T.

Math Misconception Mystery
(PAGE 2)

AFTER THE VIDEO: Discuss and analyze their answers.

The most reasonable answer belongs to Character # _____ because

_____

_____

_____

_____

(Justify how this character's work makes sense.)

Let's help the others:

	Character #___:	Character #___:	Character #___:
What did this character do that was correct?			
Identify their error			
What do they need to know to understand for next time?			

158

© McCarthy Math Academy

TAKING ON THE B.E.S.T.

 Video Lesson

The Commutative and Associative Property of Multiplication

Use the expressions below to model the following Properties of Multiplication. Include visual models.

Commutative Property of Multiplication	1. 3 x 5	2. 6 x 7
Associative Property of Multiplication	3. 2 x 3 x 4	4. 6 x 1 x 5

159

© McCarthy Math Academy

TAKING ON THE B.E.S.T.

Use the expressions below to model the following Properties of Multiplication. Include visual models.

Commutative Property of Multiplication	1 5 x 6	2 12 x 4
Associative Property of Multiplication	3 1 x 8 x 6	4 6 x 4 x 3

© McCarthy Math Academy

TAKING ON THE B.E.S.T.

  Video Lesson | The Distributive Property of Multiplication (One Digit Factors)

Break apart one factor to model the Distributive Property of Multiplication. Represent your thinking with an array.

1 3 x 6

2 7 x 7

3 9 x 4

© McCarthy Math Academy

TAKING ON THE B.E.S.T.

Break apart one factor to model the Distributive Property of Multiplication. Represent your thinking with an array.

1. 4 x 7

2. 8 x 7

3. 6 x 9

© McCarthy Math Academy

TAKING ON THE B.E.S.T.

  **Video Lesson** **The Distributive Property of Multiplication (One Digit x Two Digits)**

Break apart the two-digit factor to model the Distributive Property of Multiplication.

1 3 x 64

2 5 x 79

3 81 x 6

163

© McCarthy Math Academy

TAKING ON THE B.E.S.T.

Break apart the two-digit factor to model the Distributive Property of Multiplication.

1 2 x 47

2 4 x 55

3 7 x 18

© McCarthy Math Academy

TAKING ON THE B.E.S.T.

  Video Lesson | The Distributive Property of Multiplication (One Digit x Two Digits)

Determine the missing value, **n.** Explain your thinking.

1 $4 \times 65 = (4 \times n) + (4 \times 5)$

2 $n \times 16 = (2 \times 10) + (2 \times 6)$

3 $7 \times n = (7 \times 50) + (7 \times 9)$

© McCarthy Math Academy

TAKING ON THE B.E.S.T.

Determine the missing value, **n**. Explain your thinking.

1 $9 \times 82 = (9 \times n) + (9 \times 2)$

2 $n \times 21 = (3 \times 20) + (3 \times 1)$

3 $5 \times n = (5 \times 30) + (5 \times 3)$

166

© McCarthy Math Academy

TAKING ON THE B.E.S.T.

MA.3.AR.I.I | **Math Missions** | **Properties of Multiplication**

PART ONE

Use the expression 6 x 8 to model the Commutative Property of Multiplication. Include visual models.

PART TWO

Trent uses the expression 6 x 8 to create the expressions below. Use the Associative Property of Multiplication to prove that all expressions have the same value.

6 x (2 x 4)	(6 x 2) x 4	(2 x 4) x 6	(6 x 4) x 2

PART THREE

Show how you can use the Distributive Property of Multiplication to break down one factor to make 6 x 8 easier to solve.

© McCarthy Math Academy

TAKING ON THE B.E.S.T.

MA.3.AR.1.1 | Math Misconception Mystery (PAGE 1)

BEFORE THE VIDEO: Solve the problem on your own.

> How can you use the Distributive Property of Multiplication to multiply 8 x 47?

DURING THE VIDEO: Pause after each "character" solves the problem and jot down quick notes to help you remember what they did correctly or incorrectly.

Character #1 _____	Character #2 _____
Character #3 _____	Character #4 _____

168

© McCarthy Math Academy

TAKING ON THE B.E.S.T.

MA.3.AR.l.l

Math Misconception Mystery
(PAGE 2)

AFTER THE VIDEO: Discuss and analyze their answers.

The most reasonable answer belongs to Character # _____ because

_____

_____

_____

_____

(Justify how this character's work makes sense.)

Let's help the others:

	Character #___:	Character #___:	Character #___:
What did this character do that was correct?			
Identify their error			
What do they need to know to understand for next time?			

169

THE FANTASTIC FOUR OPERATIONS

ADDITION

?

"Join Together"

SUBTRACTION

?

"Separate"

"Compare"

"Part – Whole"

?

MULTIPLICATION

"Groups of Equal Things"

= = = =

DIVISION

"Distribute Equally"

© McCarthy Math Academy

TAKING ON THE B.E.S.T.

Questions to Consider
- ☐ What is **HAPPENING** in this problem?
- ☐ What am I trying to **FIGURE OUT**?
- ☐ What does each **QUANTITY** represent?
- ☐ Does my answer **MAKE SENSE**?

Helpful Tips:
- ☐ Read the problem **THREE** times.
- ☐ **DRAW** it out until it makes sense to you

1 Xavier plants 4 rows of tomato plants. In each row, he plants 8 tomato plants. How many tomato plants does Xavier plant?

2 A train car carries 900 pounds of lumber to a city 300 miles away. When the train arrives at the station, 644 pounds of lumber is removed from the train car. How much lumber remains?

© McCarthy Math Academy

TAKING ON THE B.E.S.T.

MA.3.AR.1.2 | Extra Practice #1 | One Step Real World Problems

Questions to Consider
- ❑ What is **HAPPENING** in this problem?
- ❑ What am I trying to **FIGURE OUT**?
- ❑ What does each **QUANTITY** represent?
- ❑ Does my answer **MAKE SENSE**?

Helpful Tips:
- ❑ Read the problem **THREE** times.
- ❑ **DRAW** it out until it makes sense to you

1 Frankie collects 198 stickers throughout the year. For his birthday, his aunt gives him a gift of 58 stickers. How many stickers does he have now?

2 Ruby has 21 pieces of fruit. She separates the fruit into 7 piles. How many pieces of fruit are in each pile?

172

TAKING ON THE B.E.S.T.

Questions to Consider
- ☐ What is **HAPPENING** in this problem?
- ☐ What am I trying to **FIGURE OUT**?
- ☐ What does each **QUANTITY** represent?
- ☐ Does my answer **MAKE SENSE**?

Helpful Tips:
- ☐ Read the problem **THREE** times.
- ☐ **DRAW** it out until it makes sense to you

---

1 Mrs. Dee is setting up the media center for the Book Fair. She arranges 8 tables around the media center and places 12 books on each table. The students in the first class purchase 9 of the books. How many books are still available for purchase?

---

2 A mechanic must replace the tires on six vehicles. Two of the vehicles have 6 tires, while the rest have 4 tires. How many tires must the mechanic replace?

173

© McCarthy Math Academy

TAKING ON THE B.E.S.T.

MA.3.AR.1.2 | **Extra Practice #2** | **Two Step Real World Problems**

Questions to Consider
- ☐ What is **HAPPENING** in this problem?
- ☐ What am I trying to **FIGURE OUT**?
- ☐ What does each **QUANTITY** represent?
- ☐ Does my answer **MAKE SENSE**?

Helpful Tips:
- ☐ Read the problem **THREE** times.
- ☐ **DRAW** it out until it makes sense to you

1 Mrs. Dee is setting up the media center for the Book Fair. She has 24 picture books and 12 chapter books to arrange equally onto four tables. How many books does she need to place on each table?

2 A mechanic has 50 tires to replace today. He has already replaced the tires on eight vehicles that needed all 4 tires replaced. How many more tires must he replace?

© McCarthy Math Academy

TAKING ON THE B.E.S.T.

MA.3.AR.1.2 | **Math Missions** | **Real World Problems Using All Four Operations**

PART ONE

Use the model below to create a real world problem. Include the scenario and a question that needs to be solved.

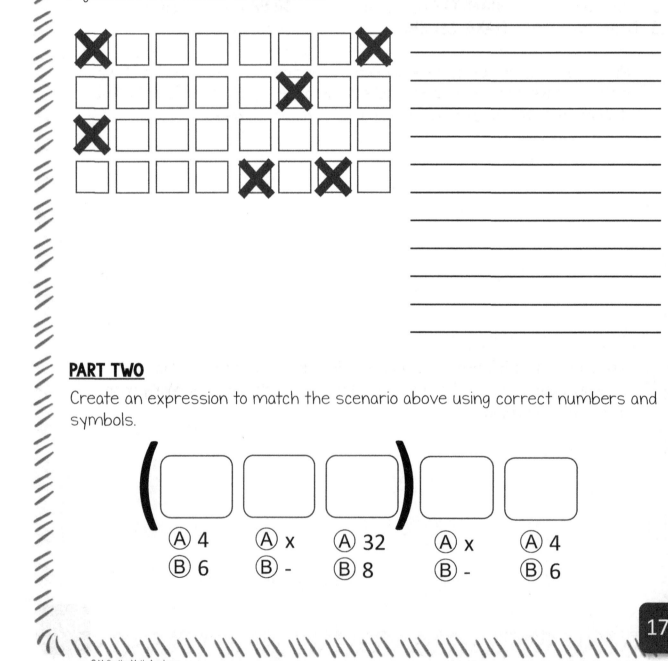

_____

_____

_____

_____

_____

_____

_____

_____

_____

_____

PART TWO

Create an expression to match the scenario above using correct numbers and symbols.

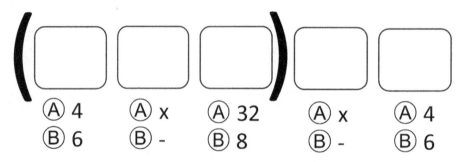

(⬜ ⬜ ⬜) ⬜ ⬜

Ⓐ 4   Ⓐ x   Ⓐ 32   Ⓐ x   Ⓐ 4
Ⓑ 6   Ⓑ -   Ⓑ 8   Ⓑ -   Ⓑ 6

© McCarthy Math Academy

TAKING ON THE B.E.S.T.

MA.3.AR.I.2 | **Math Misconception Mystery (PAGE I)**

BEFORE THE VIDEO: Solve the problem on your own.

> Gavin receives $100 for his birthday. He buys four shirts for $9 each. How much money does he have now?

DURING THE VIDEO: Pause after each "character" solves the problem and jot down quick notes to help you remember what they did correctly or incorrectly.

Character #1 _____	Character #2 _____
Character #3 _____	**Character #4** _____

© McCarthy Math Academy

TAKING ON THE B.E.S.T.

MA.3.AR.I.2 | Math Misconception Mystery (PAGE 2)

AFTER THE VIDEO: Discuss and analyze their answers.

The most reasonable answer belongs to Character # _____ because

_____

_____

_____

_____

(Justify how this character's work makes sense.)

Let's help the others:

	Character #___:	Character #___:	Character #___:
What did this character do that was correct?			
Identify their error			
What do they need to know to understand for next time?			

© McCarthy Math Academy

TAKING ON THE B.E.S.T.

  Video Lesson | **Division as a Missing Factor Problem (Array)**

Restate each division problem as a missing factor problem. Represent each with an array to show the related multiplication and division facts.

1 $15 \div 3 = n$

Restate as a missing factor problem:

Array	Other Related Facts

2 $24 \div 6 = n$

Restate as a missing factor problem:

Array	Other Related Facts

3 $36 \div 12 = n$

Restate as a missing factor problem:

Array	Other Related Facts

178

© McCarthy Math Academy

MA.3.AR.2.1 | **Extra Practice #1** | **Division as a Missing Factor Problem (Array)**

Restate each division problem as a missing factor problem. Represent each with an array to show the related multiplication and division facts.

1 $16 \div 2 = n$

Restate as a missing factor problem:

Array	Other Related Facts

2 $20 \div 4 = n$

Restate as a missing factor problem:

Array	Other Related Facts

3 $30 \div 10 = n$

Restate as a missing factor problem:

Array	Other Related Facts

© McCarthy Math Academy

TAKING ON THE B.E.S.T.

Restate each division problem as a missing factor problem. Represent each with skip counting to show the related multiplication and division facts.

---

1 $42 \div 6 = n$

Restate as a missing factor problem:

Skip Counting	Other Related Facts

---

2 $32 \div 8 = n$

Restate as a missing factor problem:

Skip Counting	Other Related Facts

---

3 $36 \div 6 = n$

Restate as a missing factor problem:

Skip Counting	Other Related Facts

© McCarthy Math Academy

TAKING ON THE B.E.S.T.

MA.3.AR.2.1	Extra Practice #2	Division as a Missing Factor Problem (Skip Counting)

Restate each division problem as a missing factor problem. Represent each with skip counting to show the related multiplication and division facts.

1 $48 \div 6 = n$

Restate as a missing factor problem:

Skip Counting	Other Related Facts

2 $10 \div 2 = n$

Restate as a missing factor problem:

Skip Counting	Other Related Facts

3 $44 \div 11 = n$

Restate as a missing factor problem:

Skip Counting	Other Related Facts

© McCarthy Math Academy

TAKING ON THE B.E.S.T.

MA.3.AR.2.1 | **Math Missions** | **Multiplication and Division are Inverse Operations**

PART ONE

Use the array below to create ONE division equation. Use the letter *n* to represent the quotient.

Create one division equation:

PART TWO

Write a multiplication equation that can be used to find the quotient. Use *n* to represent the unknown factor.

PART THREE

What is the quotient?

PART FOUR

List the other related multiplication and division equations below.

© McCarthy Math Academy

MA.3.AR.2.1 | Math Misconception Mystery (PAGE 1)

BEFORE THE VIDEO: Solve the problem on your own.

Select all of the equations that can be used to find the quotient of 63 ÷ 9.

A) 9 x ? = 63

B) 63 x 9 = ?

C) 63 x ? = 9

D) ? x 63 = 9

E) ? x 9 = 63

DURING THE VIDEO: Pause after each "character" solves the problem and jot down quick notes to help you remember what they did correctly or incorrectly.

Character #1 _____

Character #2 _____

Character #3 _____

Character #4 _____

183

© McCarthy Math Academy

TAKING ON THE B.E.S.T.

Math Misconception Mystery (PAGE 2)

AFTER THE VIDEO: Discuss and analyze their answers.

The most reasonable answer belongs to Character # _____ because

_____

_____

_____

_____

(Justify how this character's work makes sense.)

Let's help the others:			
	Character #___:	Character #___:	Character #___:
What did this character do that was correct?			
Identify their error			
What do they need to know to understand for next time?			

184

© McCarthy Math Academy

MA.3.AR.2.2  **Video Lesson** | **True or False Equations with Multiplication & Division (3 Terms)**

Explain why the equation is true or false.

1 $16 = 4 \times 5$

1 $7 = 14 \div 2$

1 $24 = 8 \times 4$

© McCarthy Math Academy

TAKING ON THE B.E.S.T.

MA.3.AR.2.2 | **Extra Practice #1** | **True or False Equations with Multiplication & Division (3 Terms)**

Explain why the equation is true or false.

1 $20 = 10 \times 2$

2 $9 = 27 \div 3$

3 $42 = 8 \times 6$

© McCarthy Math Academy

TAKING ON THE B.E.S.T.

Explain why the equation is true or false.

1 $35 \div 7 = 0 \times 5$

2 $8 \times 3 = 24 \div 3$

3 $12 \times 3 = 6 \times 6$

© McCarthy Math Academy

TAKING ON THE B.E.S.T.

Explain why the equation is true or false.

1 $56 \div 7 = 2 \times 4$

2 $81 \div 9 = 32 \div 4$

3 $12 \times 12 = 144 \div 12$

188

TAKING ON THE B.E.S.T.

| MA.3.AR.2.2 | Math Missions | True or False Equations |

Use the cards below to complete each task. You can use the cards more than once.

CARDS

| 2 | 3 | 4 | 5 | 6 | 8 | 10 | 12 |

PART ONE

Place the numbers in the cards below to create an equation that is false. Explain how you know that it is false.

$$\boxed{} \times \boxed{} = \boxed{} \div \boxed{}$$

_____

_____

_____

_____

PART TWO

Place the numbers in the cards below to create an equation that is true. Explain how you know that it is true.

$$\boxed{} \times \boxed{} = \boxed{} \div \boxed{}$$

_____

_____

_____

_____

© McCarthy Math Academy

TAKING ON THE B.E.S.T.

Math Misconception Mystery
(PAGE 1)

BEFORE THE VIDEO: Solve the problem on your own.

Which of the following describes the equation $28 \div 4 = 7 \times 0$?
Ⓐ The equation is true because the expressions on each side have a quotient of 7.
Ⓑ The equation is true because the expressions on each side have a product of 7.
Ⓒ The equation is false because the product on the left is 7, and the quotient on the right 0.
Ⓓ The equation is false because the quotient on the left is 7, and the product on the right is 0.

DURING THE VIDEO: Pause after each "character" solves the problem and jot down quick notes to help you remember what they did correctly or incorrectly.

Character #1 _____	Character #2 _____
Character #3 _____	**Character #4** _____

© McCarthy Math Academy

TAKING ON THE B.E.S.T.

Math Misconception Mystery
(PAGE 2)

AFTER THE VIDEO: Discuss and analyze their answers.

The most reasonable answer belongs to Character # _____ because

_____

_____

_____

_____

(Justify how this character's work makes sense.)

Let's help the others:

	Character #___:	Character #___:	Character #___:
What did this character do that was correct?			
Identify their error			
What do they need to know to understand for next time?			

191

© McCarthy Math Academy

TAKING ON THE B.E.S.T.

MA.3.AR.2.3 |  Video Lesson | **Determine the Unknown in a Multiplication Equation**

Determine the value of each unknown number. Then, list the related facts in the fact family.

1 $8 \times n = 16$

2 $36 = n \times 6$

3 $n = 10 \times 4$

© McCarthy Math Academy

TAKING ON THE B.E.S.T.

Determine the value of each unknown number. Then, list the related facts in the fact family.

1 $9 \times n = 45$

2 $42 = n \times 7$

$n = 3 \times 5$

© McCarthy Math Academy

TAKING ON THE B.E.S.T.

Determine the value of each unknown number. Then, list the related facts in the fact family.

1 $32 \div n = 8$

2 $12 = 60 \div n$

3 $3 = n \div 3$

194

© McCarthy Math Academy

TAKING ON THE B.E.S.T.

Extra Practice #2 **Determine the Unknown in a Division Equation**

Determine the value of each unknown number. Then, list the related facts in the fact family.

1 $64 \div n = 8$

2 $2 = 24 \div n$

$4 = n \div 6$

195

TAKING ON THE B.E.S.T.

MA.3.AR.2.3	Math Missions	Determine Unknown Values in Multiplication and Division Equations

PART ONE

Alice is struggling to decide whether the value of the unknown number in the equation below is 3 or 12. Which number is correct? Explain your thinking on the lines below.

$$6 = n \div 2$$

_____

_____

_____

_____

PART TWO

Use the equation in PART ONE to list all of the related facts.

PART THREE

Create a real-world problem to represent the situation in PART ONE. Make sure your problem includes a question to figure out the value of the unknown number.

_____

_____

_____

_____

© McCarthy Math Academy

TAKING ON THE B.E.S.T.

MA.3.AR.2.3 | Math Misconception Mystery (PAGE 1)

BEFORE THE VIDEO: Solve the problem on your own.

> What is the value of the unknown number in the equation $8 = n \div 4$?

DURING THE VIDEO: Pause after each "character" solves the problem and jot down quick notes to help you remember what they did correctly or incorrectly.

Character #1 _____

Character #2 _____

Character #3 _____

Character #4 _____

197

© McCarthy Math Academy

TAKING ON THE B.E.S.T.

Math Misconception Mystery (PAGE 2)

AFTER THE VIDEO: Discuss and analyze their answers.

The most reasonable answer belongs to Character # _____ because

_____

_____

_____

_____

(Justify how this character's work makes sense.)

Let's help the others:

	Character #___:	Character #___:	Character #___:
What did this character do that was correct?			
Identify their error			
What do they need to know to understand for next time?			

© McCarthy Math Academy

MA.3.AR.3.1  Video Lesson | **Odd or Even**

1 What are the first 10 multiples of 2?

If the ones digit in any number is a multiple of 2, it is_____.

If the ones digit in any number is not a multiple of 2, it is _____.

2 Is the number 281 even or odd? Explain how you know.

3 Is the number 67 even or odd? Explain how you know.

4 Is the number 1,000 even or odd? Explain how you know.

199

© McCarthy Math Academy

TAKING ON THE B.E.S.T.

1 Is the number 363 even or odd? Explain how you know.

2 Is the number 970 even or odd? Explain how you know.

3 Create an even number that has three digits.

4 Create an odd number that has two digits.

© McCarthy Math Academy

TAKING ON THE B.E.S.T.

MA.3.AR.3.1	Math Missions	Odd or Even

PART ONE

Use the cards to create four numbers that have three digits each. Two of the numbers must be odd and two of the numbers must be even.

CARDS

$$\boxed{1} \quad \boxed{5} \quad \boxed{6}$$

ODD

☐ ☐ ☐

☐ ☐ ☐

EVEN

☐ ☐ ☐

☐ ☐ ☐

PART TWO

Kelly creates the number 823. She says this number is even because the digits 8 and 2 are both even. Explain why Kelly's thinking is incorrect.

_____

_____

_____

_____

© McCarthy Math Academy

TAKING ON THE B.E.S.T.

MA.3.AR.3.1 | **Math Misconception Mystery (PAGE 1)**

BEFORE THE VIDEO: Solve the problem on your own.

Determine whether the numbers are even or odd in the table below.

	EVEN	ODD
74		
213		
1,000		

DURING THE VIDEO: Pause after each "character" solves the problem and jot down quick notes to help you remember what they did correctly or incorrectly.

Character #1 _____

Character #2 _____

Character #3 _____

Character #4 _____

© McCarthy Math Academy

TAKING ON THE B.E.S.T.

Math Misconception Mystery
(PAGE 2)

AFTER THE VIDEO: Discuss and analyze their answers.

The most reasonable answer belongs to Character # _____ because

_____

_____

_____

_____

(Justify how this character's work makes sense.)

Let's help the others:

	Character #___:	Character #___:	Character #___:
What did this character do that was correct?			
Identify their error			
What do they need to know to understand for next time?			

203

© McCarthy Math Academy

TAKING ON THE B.E.S.T.

MA.3.AR.3.2  Video Lesson **Multiples**

1 Is 28 a multiple of 7? Explain how you know.

2 Is 22 a multiple of 3? Explain how you know.

3 Is 42 a multiple of 4? Explain how you know.

204

© McCarthy Math Academy

1 Is 10 a multiple of 3? Explain how you know.

2 Is 33 a multiple of 3? Explain how you know.

3 Is 36 a multiple of 4? Explain how you know.

© McCarthy Math Academy

TAKING ON THE B.E.S.T.

1 Is 18 a multiple of 4? Explain how you know.

2 Is 54 a multiple of 6? Explain how you know.

3 Is 56 a multiple of 9? Explain how you know.

© McCarthy Math Academy

TAKING ON THE B.E.S.T.

| Math Missions | **Multiples**

Fill in the blanks using the cards.

CARDS

| 2 | 3 | 4 | 5 | 6 | 7 |

PART ONE

24 is a multiple of ☐ , ☐ , ☐ , and ☐ .

24 is NOT a multiple of ☐ and ☐ .

PART TWO

Determine whether 32 is a multiple of 3. Explain your thinking.

_____

_____

_____

_____

© McCarthy Math Academy

TAKING ON THE B.E.S.T.

MA.3.AR.3.2 | Math Misconception Mystery (PAGE 1)

BEFORE THE VIDEO: Solve the problem on your own.

Select all the numbers below that are NOT multiples of 6.

- (A) 6
- (B) 8
- (C) 12
- (D) 16
- (E) 18
- (F) 22

DURING THE VIDEO: Pause after each "character" solves the problem and jot down quick notes to help you remember what they did correctly or incorrectly.

Character #1 _____	Character #2 _____
Character #3 _____	**Character #4** _____

208

© McCarthy Math Academy

TAKING ON THE B.E.S.T.

Math Misconception Mystery
(PAGE 2)

AFTER THE VIDEO: Discuss and analyze their answers.

The most reasonable answer belongs to Character # _____ because

_____

_____

_____

_____

(Justify how this character's work makes sense.)

Let's help the others:

	Character #___:	Character #___:	Character #___:
What did this character do that was correct?			
Identify their error			
What do they need to know to understand for next time?			

209

© McCarthy Math Academy

TAKING ON THE B.E.S.T.

  Video Lesson **Identify Patterns**

---

1 A pattern is shown below.

4, 8, 12, 16, ...

What are TWO possible rules for the pattern?

---

2 A pattern is shown below.

33, 26, 19, 12, ...

What are TWO possible rules for the pattern?

---

3 A pattern is shown below.

1, 2, 4, 8, 16,....

What is the rule for this pattern?

© McCarthy Math Academy

TAKING ON THE B.E.S.T.

1 A pattern is shown below.

600, 577, 554, 531, ...

What are TWO possible rules for the pattern?

2 A pattern is shown below.

1, 10, 100, 1000, ...

What is the rule for this pattern?

3 A pattern is shown below.

6, 12, 18, 24, ...

What are TWO possible rules for the pattern?

© McCarthy Math Academy

TAKING ON THE B.E.S.T.

MA.3.AR.3.3  Video Lesson Create Patterns

1 Create a pattern with 5 terms that starts at 500 and has a rule of "subtract 49."

2 Create a pattern with 3 terms that starts at 24 and has a rule of "divide by 2."

3 Create a pattern with 4 terms that starts at 139 and has a rule of "add 28."

212

© McCarthy Math Academy

TAKING ON THE B.E.S.T.

| Create Patterns

1 Create a pattern with 4 terms that starts at 400 and has a rule of "subtract 68."

2 Create a pattern with 3 terms that starts at 48 and has a rule of "divide by 4."

3 Create a pattern with 4 terms that starts at 240 and has a rule of "add 35."

© McCarthy Math Academy

TAKING ON THE B.E.S.T.

MA.3.AR.3.3  Video Lesson | **Extend Patterns**

---

1 A pattern is shown below.

4, 9, 14, 19, ___ , ___ , ___

What are the next three terms in the pattern? Explain how you know.

---

2 A pattern is shown below.

500, 450, 400, 350, ___ , ___ , ___ , ___

What are the next four terms in the pattern? Explain how you know.

---

3 A pattern is shown below.

1, 3, 9, ___

What is the next term in the pattern? Explain how you know.

214

© McCarthy Math Academy

TAKING ON THE B.E.S.T.

MA.3.AR.3.3 | Extra Practice #3 | **Extend Patterns**

1 A pattern is shown below.

701, 602, 503, 404, ___ , ___ , ___ , ___

What are the next four terms in the pattern? Explain how you know.

2 A pattern is shown below.

7, 14, 21, ___ , ___ , ___

What are the next three terms in the pattern? Explain how you know.

3 A pattern is shown below.

3, 6, 12, ___

What is the next term in the pattern? Explain how you know.

© McCarthy Math Academy

TAKING ON THE B.E.S.T.

| MA.3.AR.3.3 | Math Missions | Identify, Create, and Extend Patterns |

PART ONE

Jose reads 10 pages a day. How many pages will he have read by the 12th day? Explain your thinking.

_____

_____

_____

_____

PART TWO

Katie reads 11 pages a day. How many more pages will Katie read after 12 days compared to Jose?

_____

_____

_____

_____

© McCarthy Math Academy

TAKING ON THE B.E.S.T.

MA.3.AR.3.3 | Math Misconception Mystery (PAGE 1)

BEFORE THE VIDEO: Solve the problem on your own.

What are the sixth and seventh terms of the sequence below that follows the rule "subtract 8"?

100, 92, 84, 76, ...

DURING THE VIDEO: Pause after each "character" solves the problem and jot down quick notes to help you remember what they did correctly or incorrectly.

Character #1 _____

Character #2 _____

Character #3 _____

Character #4 _____

© McCarthy Math Academy

TAKING ON THE B.E.S.T.

MA.3.AR.3.3 | Math Misconception Mystery (PAGE 2)

AFTER THE VIDEO: Discuss and analyze their answers.

The most reasonable answer belongs to Character # _____ because

_____

_____

_____

_____

(Justify how this character's work makes sense.)

Let's help the others:

	Character #___:	Character #___:	Character #___:
What did this character do that was correct?			
Identify their error			
What do they need to know to understand for next time?			

218

© McCarthy Math Academy

TAKING ON THE B.E.S.T.

MA.3.M.1.1 ·  Video Lesson · **Measuring Length**

---

1 List tools that are appropriate for measuring the length of an object.

---

2 What is the length of each object to the nearest centimeter?

C

B

A

```
0 cm  1   2   3   4   5   6   7   8   9   10   11   12
```

A: _____   B: _____   C: _____

This ruler is not drawn to scale.

---

3 What is the length of each object to the nearest quarter of an inch?

C

B

A

```
0 in   1      2      3      4      5      6
```

This ruler is not drawn to scale.

A: _____   B: _____   C: _____

© McCarthy Math Academy

TAKING ON THE B.E.S.T.

1 What is the length of each object to the nearest centimeter?

C ▬▬▬▬▬▬▬▬▬▬▬▬▬

B ▬▬▬▬▬▬▬▬

A ▬▬▬▬▬▬▬▬▬

```
0 cm  1   2   3   4   5   6   7   8   9   10  11  12
```

A: _____   B: _____   C: _____

This ruler is not drawn to scale.

2 What is the length of each object to the nearest quarter of an inch?

C ▬▬▬▬▬▬▬▬▬▬

B ▬▬▬▬▬▬▬▬▬▬▬

A ▬▬▬▬▬▬▬▬

```
0 in    1      2      3      4      5      6
```

A: _____   B: _____   C: _____

This ruler is not drawn to scale.

© McCarthy Math Academy

MA.3.M.I.I  **Video Lesson** **Measuring Liquid Volume**

1 List tools that are appropriate for measuring liquid volume.

2 Container A and B are both the same size, but are filled with different amounts. What is the volume of water in each container, in millimeters?

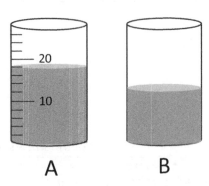

— 20

— 10

A   B

A: _ _ _ _ _ _

B: _ _ _ _ _ _

3 What is the liquid volume in the measuring cup to the nearest quarter cup?

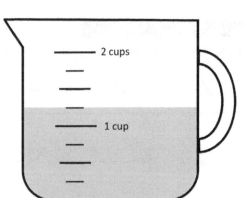

— 2 cups

— 1 cup

© McCarthy Math Academy

TAKING ON THE B.E.S.T.

| MA.3.M.1.1 | Extra Practice #2 | Measuring Liquid Volume |

1 Container A and B are both the same size, but are filled with different amounts. What is the volume of water in each container, in millimeters?

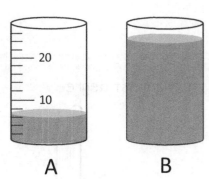

A: _____

B: _____

2 What is the liquid volume in each measuring cup to the nearest quarter cup?

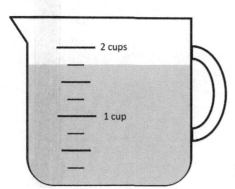

© McCarthy Math Academy

TAKING ON THE B.E.S.T.

1 List tools that are appropriate for measuring temperature.

2 Find the measure of each thermometer to the nearest degree.

A   B   C

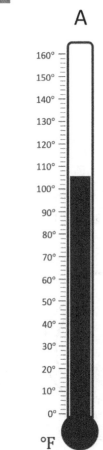
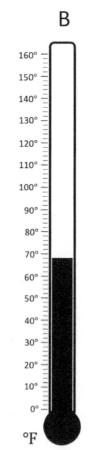

© McCarthy Math Academy

TAKING ON THE B.E.S.T.

Extra Practice #3

Measuring Temperature

Find the measure of each thermometer to the nearest degree.

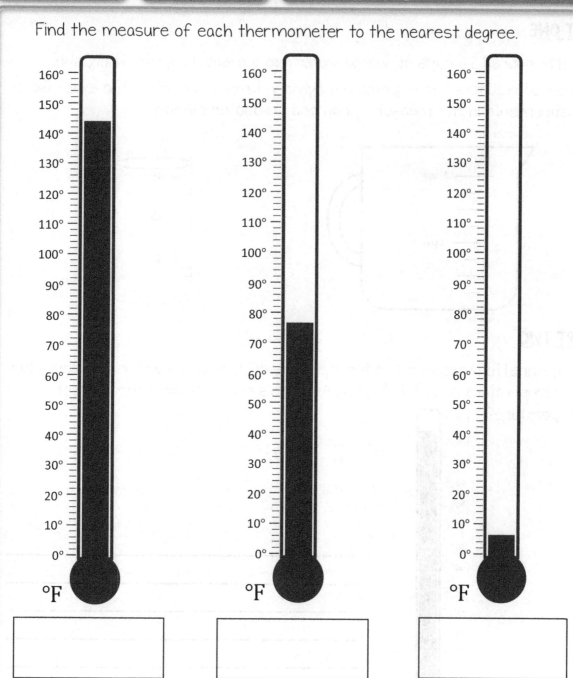

°F

°F

°F

© McCarthy Math Academy

TAKING ON THE B.E.S.T.

MA.3.M.I.I   **Math Missions**   **Measure Length, Liquid Volume, and Temperature**

PART ONE

Annette poured $1\frac{3}{4}$ cups of warm water into a measuring cup. Then, she poured 14 milliliters into a graduated cylinder. Draw a model of the exact water measurements in the measuring cup and graduated cylinder.

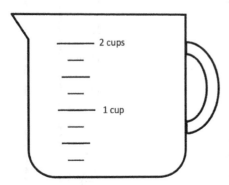
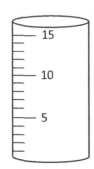

PART TWO

Next, Annette measured the temperature of the warm water. She says that the temperature is 112° F. Explain Annette's error. What is the correct temperature?

_____

_____

_____

_____

_____

_____

© McCarthy Math Academy

TAKING ON THE B.E.S.T.

Math Misconception Mystery
(PAGE 1)

BEFORE THE VIDEO: Solve the problem on your own.

What is the length of the arrow to the nearest quarter inch?

0 in   1   2   3   4   5   6

DURING THE VIDEO: Pause after each "character" solves the problem and jot down quick notes to help you remember what they did correctly or incorrectly.

Character #1 _____

Character #2 _____

Character #3 _____

Character #4 _____

© McCarthy Math Academy

TAKING ON THE B.E.S.T.

Math Misconception Mystery
(PAGE 2)

AFTER THE VIDEO: Discuss and analyze their answers.

The most reasonable answer belongs to Character # _____ because

_____

_____

_____

_____

(Justify how this character's work makes sense.)

Let's help the others:

	Character #___:	Character #___:	Character #___:
What did this character do that was correct?			
Identify their error			
What do they need to know to understand for next time?			

227

© McCarthy Math Academy

TAKING ON THE B.E.S.T.

  **Video Lesson** **Real-World Problems with Measurement**

1 A football field is 100 yards. If a football player runs 54 yards before he is tackled, how much further must he run to travel the full length of the football field?

2 Gail is making a recipe that calls for 8 cups of water. She makes four batches of the recipe in the morning and two more in the evening. How many cups of water does Gail use?

3 In the morning, the temperature in Orlando, Florida is 61°F. By the afternoon, the temperature climbs to 90°F. How much did the temperature rise from the morning to the afternoon?

© McCarthy Math Academy

TAKING ON THE B.E.S.T.

1 A grocery store employee stocks the produce department with bags of potatoes. He places 9 bags of potatoes on a stand. Each bag weighs 6 pounds. During the morning shift, 3 customers each purchase a bag of potatoes. How many pounds of potatoes remain on the stand?

2 For a large family reunion, picnic tables are lined up with a total length of 18 meters. If each picnic table has a length of 2 meters, how many picnic tables are lined up for the reunion?

3 A scientist fills six beakers with 12 milliliters of water in each. Then, she fills a graduated cylinder with 10 milliliters of water. How much more water does she have in the beakers than the graduated cylinder?

229

© McCarthy Math Academy

TAKING ON THE B.E.S.T.

1   A nickel weighs 5 grams. Veronica has ten nickels in her pocket. Then, she finds two more nickels on the floor. What is the total mass of the nickels?

2   Water boils at 100 degrees Celsius. The temperature of Kari's water is currently 78 degrees Celsius. How many more degrees does the water need to increase to reach its boiling point?

3   A business is fencing in two separate, rectangular pieces of land. Both locations have a length of 12 feet. The first has width of 8 feet. The second has a width of 9 feet. What is the total amount of fencing the business will need to fence in the perimeters of both pieces of land?

230

© McCarthy Math Academy

TAKING ON THE B.E.S.T.

Lakeside Elementary students collect cans of food to donate to a local food shelter. Below is a table to describe how many pounds of food each grade level has collected. Answer the questions based on the table.

GRADE LEVEL	POUNDS OF FOOD COLLECTED
Kindergarten	1,435
First	1,547
Second	2,801
Third	2,944
Fourth	1,866
Fifth	2,499

Which grade level collects the most food?

Which grade level collects the least food?

How much more does Kindergarten and First Grade collect combined than Fifth Grade?

Fourth Grade wants to collect more than Third Grade. What is the least amount of food they can collect to achieve this goal?

231

© McCarthy Math Academy

TAKING ON THE B.E.S.T.

MA.3.M.1.2 | Math Misconception Mystery (PAGE 1)

BEFORE THE VIDEO: Solve the problem on your own.

Fuad has twelve nails the same size as the one below. About how long are the nails if they are in a straight line?

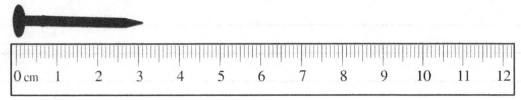

DURING THE VIDEO: Pause after each "character" solves the problem and jot down quick notes to help you remember what they did correctly or incorrectly.

Character #1 _____

Character #2 _____

Character #3 _____

Character #4 _____

© McCarthy Math Academy

TAKING ON THE B.E.S.T.

Math Misconception Mystery (PAGE 2)

AFTER THE VIDEO: Discuss and analyze their answers.

The most reasonable answer belongs to Character # _____ because

_____

_____

_____

_____

(Justify how this character's work makes sense.)

Let's help the others:

	Character #___:	Character #___:	Character #___:
What did this character do that was correct?			
Identify their error			
What do they need to know to understand for next time?			

233

© McCarthy Math Academy

TAKING ON THE B.E.S.T.

What is the difference between "AM" and "PM?"

What do the numbers on the clock represent?

"HALF PAST"
Half past 4 o'clock

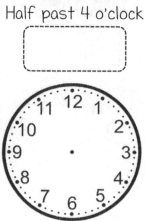

"HALF OF"
Half of 4 o'clock

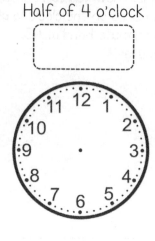

"A QUARTER PAST"
A quarter past 5 o'clock

"A QUARTER TIL"
A quarter til 5 o'clock

"A QUARTER OF"
A quarter of 2 o'clock

© McCarthy Math Academy

TAKING ON THE B.E.S.T.

MA.3.M.2.1 | **Extra Practice #1** | **Analog Clock Review**

Which meal would you most-likely eat at 6:30 AM?

Explain how you can use the numbers on the clock to place the minute hand at 48 minutes?

"HALF PAST"
Half past 12 o'clock

"HALF OF"
Half of 12 o'clock

"A QUARTER PAST"
A quarter past 3 o'clock

"A QUARTER TIL"
A quarter til 11 o'clock

"A QUARTER OF"
A quarter of 7 o'clock

235

© McCarthy Math Academy

TAKING ON THE B.E.S.T.

Determine the time on each analog clock and write it on the digital clock.

1

2

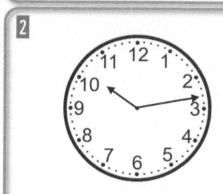

3

236

© McCarthy Math Academy

TAKING ON THE B.E.S.T.

| MA.3.M.2.1 | Extra Practice #2 | Telling Time: Analog to Digital |

Determine the time on each analog clock and write it on the digital clock.

1

2

3

© McCarthy Math Academy

TAKING ON THE B.E.S.T.

 Video Lesson

Telling Time: Digital to Analog

Use the time shown on the digital clock to draw the time on the analog clock.

1

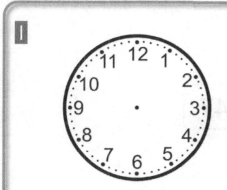

8 : 23

2

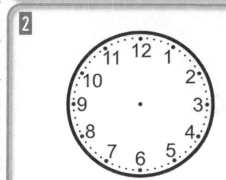

11 : 19

3

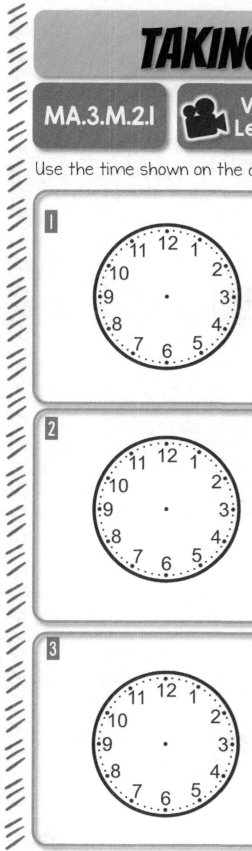

1 : 36

238

© McCarthy Math Academy

TAKING ON THE B.E.S.T.

Determine the time on each analog clock and write it on the digital clock.

1
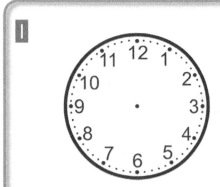

$6 : 47$

2
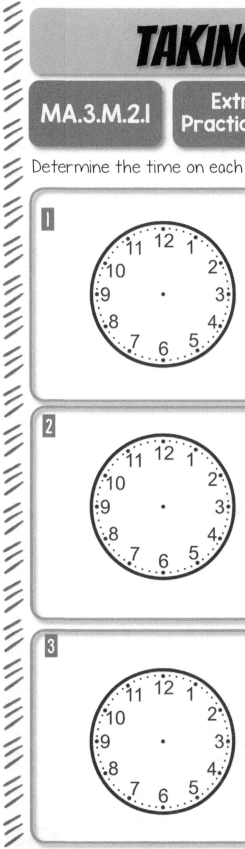

$2 : 02$

3
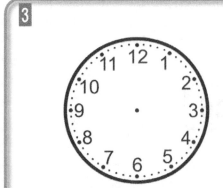

$12 : 31$

© McCarthy Math Academy

TAKING ON THE B.E.S.T.

| MA.3.M.2.1 | Math Missions | Telling Time |

The third grade classes at Pinecone Elementary go to the cafeteria for lunch according to the schedule below.

TEACHER	LUNCH TIME
Mr. Hamburg	11:15 a.m.
Mrs. Strawberry	11:18 a.m.
Ms. Octorupe	11:21 a.m.
Mr. Schumacher	11:24 a.m.

Label and model the lunch times on the clocks below.

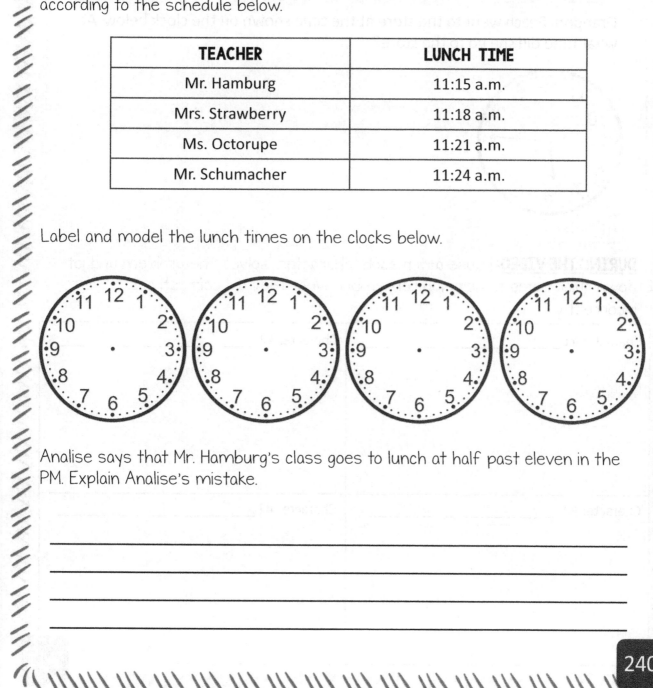

Analise says that Mr. Hamburg's class goes to lunch at half past eleven in the PM. Explain Analise's mistake.

_____

_____

_____

_____

© McCarthy Math Academy

TAKING ON THE B.E.S.T.

MA.3.M.2.1

Math Misconception Mystery
(PAGE 1)

BEFORE THE VIDEO: Solve the problem on your own.

Grandma Peach went to the store at the time shown on the clock below. At what time did she go to the store?

DURING THE VIDEO: Pause after each "character" solves the problem and jot down quick notes to help you remember what they did correctly or incorrectly.

Character #1 _____

Character #2 _____

Character #3 _____

Character #4 _____

© McCarthy Math Academy

TAKING ON THE B.E.S.T.

Math Misconception Mystery
(PAGE 2)

AFTER THE VIDEO: Discuss and analyze their answers.

The most reasonable answer belongs to Character # _____ because

_____

_____

_____

_____

(Justify how this character's work makes sense.)

Let's help the others:

	Character #___:	Character #___:	Character #___:
What did this character do that was correct?			
Identify their error			
What do they need to know to understand for next time?			

242

© McCarthy Math Academy

TAKING ON THE B.E.S.T.

1 Tucker eats breakfast at 7:13 a.m. He finishes eating breakfast at 7:32 a.m. How long does it take for Tucker to eat his breakfast?

2 Mariela begins her homework at 5:05 p.m. How long does it take for Mariela to finish her homework if she ends at 5:58 p.m.?

3 Juniper takes the cake out of the oven at 4:32 p.m. If she put the cake in at 3:54 p.m., how long did the cake bake?

© McCarthy Math Academy

TAKING ON THE B.E.S.T.

1 Tucker eats breakfast at 6:27 a.m. He finishes eating breakfast at 7:19 a.m. How long does it take for Tucker to eat his breakfast?

2 Mariela begins her homework at 4:46 p.m. How long does it take for Mariela to finish her homework if she ends at 5:56 p.m.?

3 Juniper takes the cake out of the oven at 5:49 p.m. If she put the cake in at 4:50 p.m., how long did the cake bake?

© McCarthy Math Academy

TAKING ON THE B.E.S.T.

  Video Lesson | **Determine the End Time**

1 Barney III started his stage rehearsal at 3:15 p.m. If his rehearsal lasted 37 minutes, when did it end?

2 Garfield the II cuts up tomatoes, carrots, and onions for his salad. If it takes him 18 minutes to prepare his salad and he begins at 12:53 p.m., what time does he finish?

3 A crab in South Florida travels from the mangrove trees to the shoreline. The Robertson Family tracks the time it takes for the crab to get to the shoreline. If it took him 75 minutes to get to the shoreline, and he began at 9:45 a.m., what time did he reach the shoreline?

245

© McCarthy Math Academy

TAKING ON THE B.E.S.T.

1 Barney III started his stage rehearsal at 3:31 p.m. If his rehearsal lasted 45 minutes, when did it end?

2 Garfield the II cuts up tomatoes, carrots, and onions for his salad. If it takes him 12 minutes to prepare his salad and he begins at 10:58 p.m., what time does he finish?

3 A crab in South Florida travels from the mangrove trees to the shoreline. The Robertson Family tracks the time it takes for the crab to get to the shoreline. If it took him 90 minutes to get to the shoreline, and he began at 10:27 a.m., what time did he reach the shoreline?

© McCarthy Math Academy

TAKING ON THE B.E.S.T.

MA.3.M.2.2  **Video Lesson** | **Determine the Start Time**

1 Jennifer's surf lessons last 90 minutes. If her lessons end at 4:15 p.m., what time do they begin?

2 Marshal finishes building a sandcastle at 3:34 p.m. He started building the sandcastle 45 minutes earlier. What time did he start?

3 Mrs. Hanson wakes up at 11:14 p.m. She realizes she has only been asleep for 80 minutes. What time did she fall asleep?

© McCarthy Math Academy

TAKING ON THE B.E.S.T.

1 Jennifer's surf lessons last 65 minutes. If her lessons end at 2:20 p.m., what time do they begin?

2 Marshal finishes building a sandcastle at 1:24 p.m. He started building the sandcastle 35 minutes earlier. What time did he start?

3 Mrs. Hanson wakes up at 9:20 p.m. She realizes she has only been asleep for 90 minutes. What time did she fall asleep?

248

© McCarthy Math Academy

TAKING ON THE B.E.S.T.

  Video Lesson **Multi-Step Time Problems**

1 Valerie begins a project at 8:15 a.m. She completes the project at 9:10 a.m. Her project consists of her writing social media posts for a company. If she completes a social media post every five minutes, how many social posts does she write?

2 Liam begins his race at 7:30 a.m. He runs for 45 minutes. What time does he finish his race? If he stops takes a sip of water every nine minutes, how many sips of water does he take?

3 It takes Jeff 48 minutes to clean his room. He tells his dad that he finishes cleaning at 9:16 a.m. What time does start cleaning? Jeff also plays the same song over and over while he cleans his room. The song is exactly four minutes long. How many times did he play the song?

249

© McCarthy Math Academy

TAKING ON THE B.E.S.T.

1 It takes 60 minutes for a musician to play his set at a restaurant. He dedicates 5 minutes for each song. If he ends his set at 4:30 p.m., what time does he begin his set? How many songs will he be able to play?

2 The Waltons go for a bike ride in a state park. The begin their ride at 9:05 a.m., and they ride for 36 minutes. Every four minutes, they stop to take a picture. When did they finish their bike ride, and how many pictures did they take?

3 Hung's family is on a camping trip. They sit around the campfire and place a log on the fire every nine minutes. If they light the campfire at 6:25 p.m., and they use up all nine logs, what time did they end, and how long did they sit around the campfire?

© McCarthy Math Academy

TAKING ON THE B.E.S.T.

MA.3.M.2.2 | **Math Missions** | **Elapsed Time**

Marie is training for a 5K race.

PART ONE

Every Saturday, Marie runs a 5K and tracks her time in the table below. Some of the values are missing. Use the information in the table to fill in the missing values.

DATE	START TIME	END TIME	ELAPSED TIME
March 7th	7:01 a.m.	7:59 a.m.	
March 14th	7:21 a.m.		44 minutes
March 21st		7:54 a.m.	42 minutes
March 28th	6:54 a.m.		43 minutes

PART TWO

Marie says that her fastest time was March 28th because this is the day she started running at the earliest time. Is Marie correct? Explain your reasoning.

_____

_____

_____

_____

© McCarthy Math Academy

TAKING ON THE B.E.S.T.

MA.3.M.2.2 | Math Misconception Mystery (PAGE 1)

BEFORE THE VIDEO: Solve the problem on your own.

> Manuela starts reading at the time shown on the clock below. If she reads for 54 minutes, what time does she finish reading?

DURING THE VIDEO: Pause after each "character" solves the problem and jot down quick notes to help you remember what they did correctly or incorrectly.

Character #1 _____

Character #2 _____

Character #3 _____

Character #4 _____

© McCarthy Math Academy

TAKING ON THE B.E.S.T.

Math Misconception Mystery
(PAGE 2)

AFTER THE VIDEO: Discuss and analyze their answers.

The most reasonable answer belongs to Character # _____ because

_____

_____

_____

_____

(Justify how this character's work makes sense.)

Let's help the others:

	Character #___:	Character #___:	Character #___:
What did this character do that was correct?			
Identify their error			
What do they need to know to understand for next time?			

253

© McCarthy Math Academy

Identify the correct name for each figure. Provide a brief description of each.

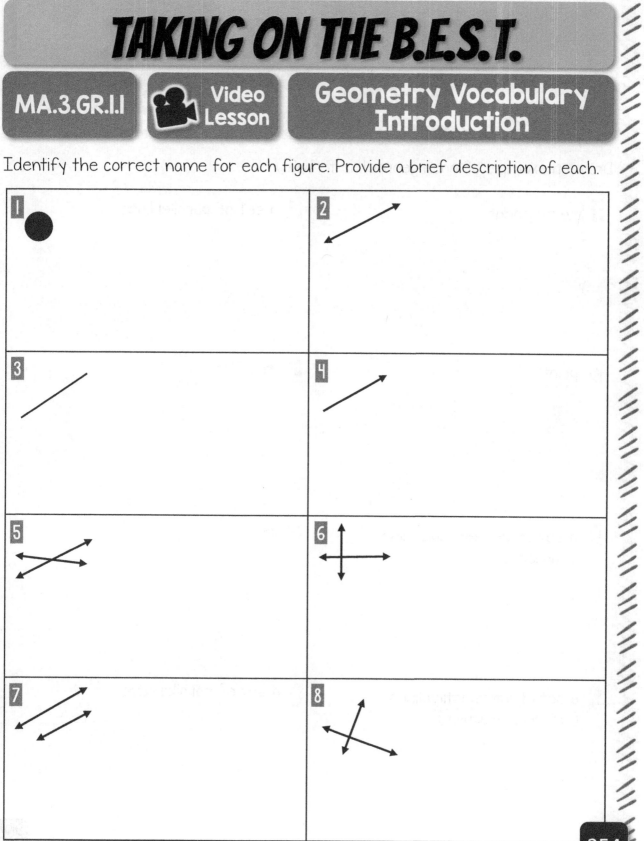

© McCarthy Math Academy

TAKING ON THE B.E.S.T.

Draw an example of each geometric term(s).

1 line segment	**2** a set of parallel lines
3 point	**4** ray
5 a set of perpendicular line segments	**6** line
7 a set of intersecting lines (not perpendicular)	**8** a set of parallel rays

255

© McCarthy Math Academy

TAKING ON THE B.E.S.T.

Determine whether each shape has the listed geometric features.

1

❑ Point(s)
❑ Line(s) or Line segment(s)
❑ Intersecting lines or line segments
❑ Perpendicular lines or line segments
❑ Parallel lines or lines or line segments

2

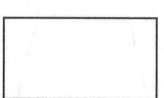

❑ Point(s)
❑ Line(s) or Line segment(s)
❑ Intersecting lines or line segments
❑ Perpendicular lines or line segments
❑ Parallel lines or lines or line segments

3

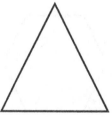

❑ Point(s)
❑ Line(s) or Line segment(s)
❑ Intersecting lines or line segments
❑ Perpendicular lines or line segments
❑ Parallel lines or lines or line segments

4

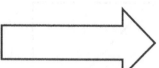

❑ Point(s)
❑ Line(s) or Line segment(s)
❑ Intersecting lines or line segments
❑ Perpendicular lines or line segments
❑ Parallel lines or lines or line segments

© McCarthy Math Academy

Determine whether each shape has the listed geometric features.

1

- ❏ Point(s)
- ❏ Line(s) or Line segment(s)
- ❏ Intersecting lines or line segments
- ❏ Perpendicular lines or line segments
- ❏ Parallel lines or lines or line segments

2

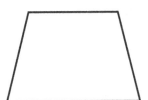

- ❏ Point(s)
- ❏ Line(s) or Line segment(s)
- ❏ Intersecting lines or line segments
- ❏ Perpendicular lines or line segments
- ❏ Parallel lines or lines or line segments

3

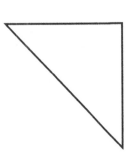

- ❏ Point(s)
- ❏ Line(s) or Line segment(s)
- ❏ Intersecting lines or line segments
- ❏ Perpendicular lines or line segments
- ❏ Parallel lines or lines or line segments

4

- ❏ Point(s)
- ❏ Line(s) or Line segment(s)
- ❏ Intersecting lines or line segments
- ❏ Perpendicular lines or line segments
- ❏ Parallel lines or lines or line segments

257

© McCarthy Math Academy

TAKING ON THE B.E.S.T.

Below is a map of the streets in a fictional city, Joyville.

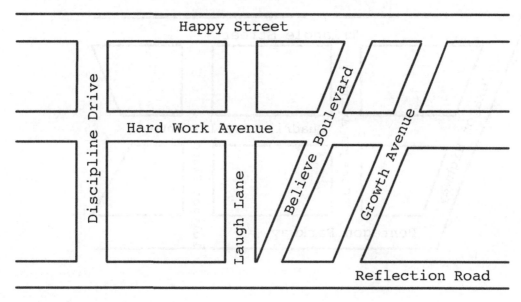

Use the map to complete the tasks below.

1 Name two roads that provide an example of **INTERSECTING** line segments.

2 Name two roads that provide an example of **PERPENDICULAR** line segments.

3 Name two roads that provide an example of **PARALLEL** line segments.

4 Name an example of a specific **POINT** on the map.

258

© McCarthy Math Academy

TAKING ON THE B.E.S.T.

MA.3.GR.1.1 | **Extra Practice #3** | **Identifying Geometric Features in Real-World Settings**

Below is a map of the streets in a fictional city, Geometry Land.

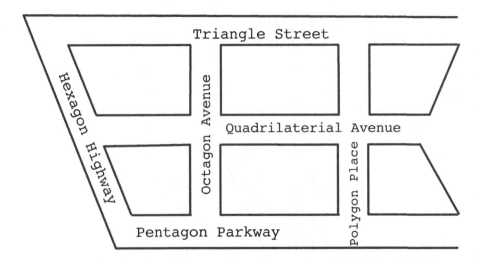

Use the map to complete the tasks below.

1 Name two roads that provide an example of **INTERSECTING** line segments.

2 Name two roads that provide an example of **PERPENDICULAR** line segments.

3 Name two roads that provide an example of **PARALLEL** line segments.

4 Name an example of a specific **POINT** on the map.

259

© McCarthy Math Academy

TAKING ON THE B.E.S.T.

MA.3.GR.1.1 | **Math Missions** | **Geometric Features**

PART ONE

Will says that intersecting lines are sometimes parallel. Do you agree or disagree with Will? Explain your thinking.

_____

_____

_____

_____

PART TWO

Chris says intersecting lines are sometimes perpendicular. Do you agree or disagree with Chris? Explain your thinking.

_____

_____

_____

PART THREE

Maya is thinking of a 4-sided polygon with only one pair of parallel lines and only one pair of perpendicular lines. Draw a figure that Maya could be thinking

© McCarthy Math Academy

TAKING ON THE B.E.S.T.

Math Misconception Mystery (PAGE 1)

BEFORE THE VIDEO: Solve the problem on your own.

> Does a rectangle always, sometimes, or never have perpendicular lines?

DURING THE VIDEO: Pause after each "character" solves the problem and jot down quick notes to help you remember what they did correctly or incorrectly.

Character #1 _____	Character #2 _____
Character #3 _____	**Character #4** _____

© McCarthy Math Academy

TAKING ON THE B.E.S.T.

Math Misconception Mystery
(PAGE 2)

AFTER THE VIDEO: Discuss and analyze their answers.

The most reasonable answer belongs to Character # _____ because

_____

_____

_____

_____

(Justify how this character's work makes sense.)

Let's help the others:

	Character #___:	Character #___:	Character #___:
What did this character do that was correct?			
Identify their error			
What do they need to know to understand for next time?			

262

© McCarthy Math Academy

TAKING ON THE B.E.S.T.

MA.3.GR.I.2 |  **Video Lesson** | **Identifying Quadrilaterals**

---

1 What is the definition of a quadrilateral?

---

2 Draw five different quadrilaterals.

---

3 Draw two non-examples of a quadrilateral. Explain why each is NOT a quadrilateral.

© McCarthy Math Academy

TAKING ON THE B.E.S.T.

Which of the following figures are quadrilaterals? Select all that apply. If a figure is NOT a quadrilateral, explain your reasoning.

A

E

B

F

C

G

D

H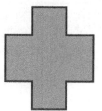

© McCarthy Math Academy

MA.3.GR.1.2  **Video Lesson** | **Quadrilaterals with 1 or 2 Pairs of Parallel Lines**

1 What is a quadrilateral with at least 1 pair of parallel sides called? Draw three examples of this type of quadrilateral.

2 What is a quadrilateral with 2 pairs of parallel sides called? Draw three examples of this type of quadrilateral.

3 What do trapezoids and parallelograms have in common? How are they different?

265

© McCarthy Math Academy

TAKING ON THE B.E.S.T.

1 Ricardo says that all of the figures below are parallelograms because they have at least one pair of parallel sides. Do you agree or disagree with Ricardo? Explain your reasoning.

_____

_____

_____

2 Penelope says that rectangles, rhombi, and squares are always parallelograms. Is Penelope correct? Explain your reasoning.

_____

_____

_____

_____

266

© McCarthy Math Academy

MA.3.GR.1.2  **Video Lesson** | **Quadrilaterals with Equal Angles and Sides**

1 What is a quadrilateral with 4 right angles called? Draw two examples of this type of quadrilateral.

2 What is a quadrilateral with 4 equal or congruent sides called ? Draw two examples of this type of quadrilateral.

2 What is a quadrilateral with 4 equal or congruent sides AND 4 right angles called? Draw two examples of this type of quadrilateral.

© McCarthy Math Academy

1. Bryce thinks that a rhombus and parallelogram are exactly the same because they both have 4 sides and two pairs of parallel sides. How can you explain their difference to Bryce?

_____

_____

_____

2. Is a rhombus always, sometimes, or never a square? Explain your thinking.

_____

_____

_____

_____

© McCarthy Math Academy

TAKING ON THE B.E.S.T.

MA.3.GR.1.2 | **Math Missions** | **Quadrilaterals**

PART ONE

Draw an example of a quadrilateral with four equal sides, but no right angles.

PART TWO

Draw an example of a quadrilateral with only one pair of parallel sides.

PART THREE

Draw an example of a quadrilateral that has four equal sides and four right angles.

269

© McCarthy Math Academy

TAKING ON THE B.E.S.T.

Math Misconception Mystery
(PAGE 1)

BEFORE THE VIDEO: Solve the problem on your own.

> Which of the following quadrilaterals always have four equal or congruent sides?
> Ⓐ rectangle
> Ⓑ square
> Ⓒ trapezoid
> Ⓓ rhombus
> Ⓔ parallelogram
> Ⓕ hexagon

DURING THE VIDEO: Pause after each "character" solves the problem and jot down quick notes to help you remember what they did correctly or incorrectly.

Character #1 _____	Character #2 _____
Character #3 _____	**Character #4** _____

270

© McCarthy Math Academy

TAKING ON THE B.E.S.T.

MA.3.GR.I.2 | Math Misconception Mystery (PAGE 2)

AFTER THE VIDEO: Discuss and analyze their answers.

The most reasonable answer belongs to Character # _____ because

_____

_____

_____

_____

(Justify how this character's work makes sense.)

Let's help the others:

	Character #___:	Character #___:	Character #___:
What did this character do that was correct?			
Identify their error			
What do they need to know to understand for next time?			

271

© McCarthy Math Academy

TAKING ON THE B.E.S.T.

📹 **Video Lesson**   **Can You Find Lines of Symmetry?**

For this video lesson, please refer to the printable page to fold the shapes to determine if it is line–symmetric or not. Then, draw the lines of symmetry that you find.

---

1 Does this shape have any lines of symmetry? If so, how many?

---

2 Does this shape have any lines of symmetry? If so, how many?

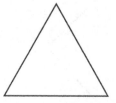

---

2 Does this shape have any lines of symmetry? If so, how many?

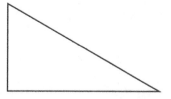

© McCarthy Math Academy

TAKING ON THE B.E.S.T.

MA.3.GR.I.3 | **Extra Practice #1** | **Can You Find Lines of Symmetry?**

For this extra practice, please refer to the printable page to fold the shapes to determine if it is line–symmetric or not. Then, draw the lines of symmetry that you find.

---

1 Does this shape have any lines of symmetry? If so, how many?

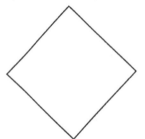

---

2 Does this shape have any lines of symmetry? If so, how many?

---

2 Does this shape have any lines of symmetry? If so, how many?

273

© McCarthy Math Academy

TAKING ON THE B.E.S.T.

For this video lesson, please refer to the printable page to fold the letters to determine if it is line-symmetric or not. Then, draw the lines of symmetry that you find.

1 Does this letter have any lines of symmetry? If so, how many?

2 Does this letter have any lines of symmetry? If so, how many?

2 Does this letter have any lines of symmetry? If so, how many?

© McCarthy Math Academy

TAKING ON THE B.E.S.T.

| Can You Find Lines of Symmetry?

For this extra practice lesson, please refer to the printable page to fold the letters to determine if it is line-symmetric or not. Then, draw the lines of symmetry that you find.

1 Does this letter have any lines of symmetry? If so, how many?

2 Does this letter have any lines of symmetry? If so, how many?

2 Does this letter have any lines of symmetry? If so, how many?

© McCarthy Math Academy

TAKING ON THE B.E.S.T.

MA.3.GR.1.3 | **Math Missions** | **Lines of Symmetry**

PART ONE

Nico says that the uppercase letter N below has one line of symmetry. Liam says that the uppercase letter N is not line–symmetric. Who is correct? Show your thinking.

N

PART TWO

Think of an uppercase letter that has more than one line of symmetry. Draw your best version of this letter. Mark the lines of symmetry to prove that it has more than one line of symmetry.

© McCarthy Math Academy

TAKING ON THE B.E.S.T.

MA.3.GR.1.3 | Math Misconception Mystery (PAGE 1)

BEFORE THE VIDEO: Solve the problem on your own.

> How many lines of symmetry does the figure have?

DURING THE VIDEO: Pause after each "character" solves the problem and jot down quick notes to help you remember what they did correctly or incorrectly.

Character #1 _____	Character #2 _____
Character #3 _____	Character #4 _____

© McCarthy Math Academy

TAKING ON THE B.E.S.T.

Math Misconception Mystery
(PAGE 2)

AFTER THE VIDEO: Discuss and analyze their answers.

The most reasonable answer belongs to Character # _____ because

_____

_____

_____

_____

(Justify how this character's work makes sense.)

Let's help the others:

	Character #___:	Character #___:	Character #___:
What did this character do that was correct?			
Identify their error			
What do they need to know to understand for next time?			

278

© McCarthy Math Academy

TAKING ON THE B.E.S.T.

1. If each unit below represents 1 square centimeter, find the area of the rectangle.

2. If each unit below represents 1 square inch, find the area of the square.

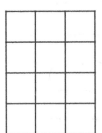

3. If each unit below represents 1 square yard, find the area of the rectangle.

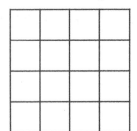

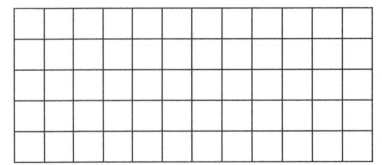

279

© McCarthy Math Academy

TAKING ON THE B.E.S.T.

1 If each unit below represents 1 square foot, find the area of the rectangle.

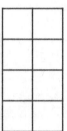

2 If each unit below represents 1 square meter, find the area of the square.

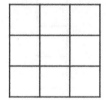

3 If each unit below represents 1 square yard, find the area of the rectangle.

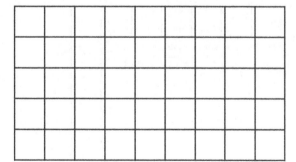

© McCarthy Math Academy

TAKING ON THE B.E.S.T.

MA.3.GR.2.1 **Video Lesson** **Finding Area by Finishing the Tiling**

1 If each unit below represents 1 square centimeter, find the area of the rectangle.

2 If each unit below represents 1 square inch, find the area of the square.

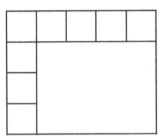

3 If each unit below represents 1 square yard, find the area of the rectangle.

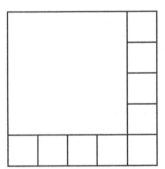

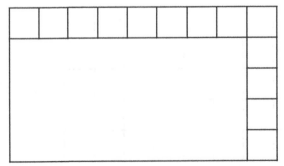

281

© McCarthy Math Academy

TAKING ON THE B.E.S.T.

| MA.3.GR.2.1 | Extra Practice #2 | Finding Area by Finishing the Tiling |

1 If each unit below represents 1 square centimeter, find the area of the rectangle.

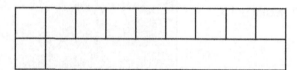

2 If each unit below represents 1 square inch, find the area of the rectangle.

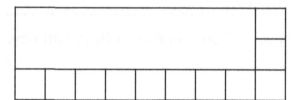

3 If each unit below represents 1 square yard, find the area of the rectangle.

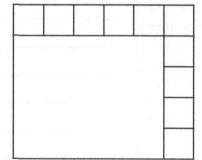

© McCarthy Math Academy

TAKING ON THE B.E.S.T.

| MA.3.GR.2.1 | Math Missions | Finding Area by Counting Squares |

Janet wants to add new tile to part of her living room. Each tile has side lengths of 1 square foot. Her design is below with the shaded area representing where she wants to add the new tiles.

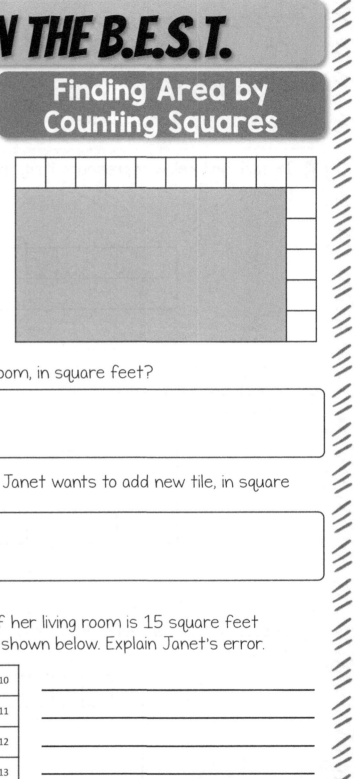

PART ONE

What is the area of the entire living room, in square feet?

What is the area of the space where Janet wants to add new tile, in square feet?

PART TWO

Janet tells her mom that the area of her living room is 15 square feet because she counted the squares as shown below. Explain Janet's error.

283

TAKING ON THE B.E.S.T.

MA.3.GR.2.1

Math Misconception Mystery
(PAGE 1)

BEFORE THE VIDEO: Solve the problem on your own.

What is the area of the rectangle below?

1 cm
1 cm

DURING THE VIDEO: Pause after each "character" solves the problem and jot down quick notes to help you remember what they did correctly or incorrectly.

Character #1 _____	Character #2 _____
Character #3 _____	Character #4 _____

284

© McCarthy Math Academy

TAKING ON THE B.E.S.T.

| **Math Misconception Mystery (PAGE 2)**

AFTER THE VIDEO: Discuss and analyze their answers.

The most reasonable answer belongs to Character # _____ because

_____

_____

_____

_____

(Justify how this character's work makes sense.)

Let's help the others:

	Character #___:	Character #___:	Character #___:
What did this character do that was correct?			
Identify their error			
What do they need to know to understand for next time?			

© McCarthy Math Academy

TAKING ON THE B.E.S.T.

1 How can you use repeated addition and multiplication to find the area of the rectangle below?

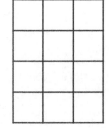

1 cm
1 cm

2 How can you use repeated addition and multiplication to find the area of the square below?

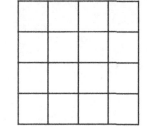

1 ft
1 ft

3 How can you use repeated addition and multiplication to find the area of the rectangle below?

1 yd
1 yd

© McCarthy Math Academy

TAKING ON THE B.E.S.T.

1. How can you use repeated addition and multiplication to find the area of the rectangle below?

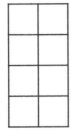

2. How can you use repeated addition and multiplication to find the area of the rectangle below?

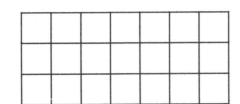

3. How can you use repeated addition and multiplication to find the area of the rectangle below?

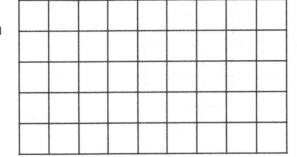

287

TAKING ON THE B.E.S.T.

1. What is the area of the rectangle below?

4 in

6 in

2. What is the area of the rectangle below?

3 ft

7 ft

3. What is the area of the square below?

8 cm

© McCarthy Math Academy

TAKING ON THE B.E.S.T.

1 What is the area of the rectangle below?

7 in

11 in

2 What is the area of the rectangle below?

4 ft

9 ft

3 What is the area of the square below?

11 cm

© McCarthy Math Academy

TAKING ON THE B.E.S.T.

PART ONE

Monique draws a rectangle that has an area of 24 square inches. Draw and label four different rectangles with dimensions that could represent Monique's rectangle.

Draw rectangle #1 here:	Draw rectangle #2 here:
Draw rectangle #3 here:	Draw rectangle #4 here:

PART TWO

Samson draws the square below to represent Monique's rectangle with an area of 24 square inches. Samson states that he "added 6+6+6+6 to get a total of 24 inches." Explain Samson's error.

6 in

6 in

_____
_____
_____
_____
_____
_____

© McCarthy Math Academy

TAKING ON THE B.E.S.T.

MA.3.GR.2.2 | Math Misconception Mystery (PAGE 1)

BEFORE THE VIDEO: Solve the problem on your own.

What is the area of the rectangle below?

12 cm

6 cm

DURING THE VIDEO: Pause after each "character" solves the problem and jot down quick notes to help you remember what they did correctly or incorrectly.

Character #1 _____

Character #2 _____

Character #3 _____

Character #4 _____

291

© McCarthy Math Academy

TAKING ON THE B.E.S.T.

Math Misconception Mystery
(PAGE 2)

AFTER THE VIDEO: Discuss and analyze their answers.

The most reasonable answer belongs to Character # _____ because

_____

_____

_____

_____

(Justify how this character's work makes sense.)

Let's help the others:

	Character #___:	Character #___:	Character #___:
What did this character do that was correct?			
Identify their error			
What do they need to know to understand for next time?			

292

© McCarthy Math Academy

TAKING ON THE B.E.S.T.

1   Ingrid has a rectangular picture frame with a length of 5 inches and a width of 7 inches. What is the perimeter of her picture frame? What is the area?

2   Mr. Jackson is adding new soil to his rectangular garden and a fence to keep the critters out. The width of his garden is 8 feet. The length of his garden is 7 feet. Find the perimeter of his garden to determine how much fencing Mr. Jackson will need. Then, find the area to determine how much soil he will need to cover the garden.

3   A square has a side length of 12 centimeters. Find the area and perimeter of the square.

© McCarthy Math Academy

TAKING ON THE B.E.S.T.

1 Avery needs to paint a wall in her house. The wall has a width of 11 feet and a length of 10 feet. Find the area of the wall in Avery's house. Then, find the perimeter.

2 Isabella is tiling the floor in kitchen. The floor is 5 feet wide and 12 feet long. What is the perimeter of Isabella's kitchen? What is the area of Isabella's kitchen?

3 A square has a side length of 9 yards. Find the area and perimeter of the square.

© McCarthy Math Academy

1 Benjamin draws a square on his paper. He uses a ruler to create straight edges. Each side has a length of 7 inches. What is the perimeter of Benjamin's square? What is the area of Benjamin's square?

2 Mrs. Mason needs to purchase a blank canvas for a new painting. She wants the length of the canvas to be 12 inches and the width to be 11 inches. Find the area of the blank canvas that Mrs. Mason is looking for. Then, determine the perimeter of her ideal canvas.

3 Jonas mows his rectangular lawn every Saturday. His front yard is enclosed by a fence that is 12 yards long and 8 yards wide. What is the perimeter of Jonas's yard? What is the area of the lawn that Jonas mows every Saturday?

© McCarthy Math Academy

TAKING ON THE B.E.S.T.

PART ONE

Sebastian wants to create a rectangular dance stage that has an area of 36 square meters. Help Sebastian determine three possibilities for building his dance stage by completing the table below.

AREA	LENGTH	WIDTH	PERIMETER
36 sq. m.			
36 sq. m.			
36 sq. m.			

PART TWO

Sebastian thinks about expanding his stage to be in the shape of a square with an area of 40 square meters. Is this possible? Explain your reasoning.

_____

_____

_____

_____

© McCarthy Math Academy

TAKING ON THE B.E.S.T.

MA.3.GR.2.3 | Math Misconception Mystery (PAGE 1)

BEFORE THE VIDEO: Solve the problem on your own.

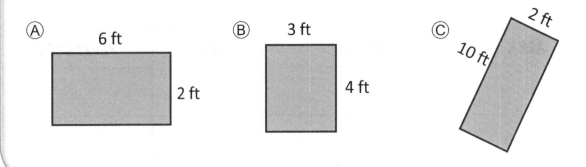

Which of the following rectangles has a perimeter of 14 feet and an area of 12 square feet?

Ⓐ 6 ft 2 ft

Ⓑ 3 ft 4 ft

Ⓒ 2 ft 10 ft

DURING THE VIDEO: Pause after each "character" solves the problem and jot down quick notes to help you remember what they did correctly or incorrectly.

Character #1 _____

Character #2 _____

Character #3 _____

Character #4 _____

© McCarthy Math Academy

TAKING ON THE B.E.S.T.

Math Misconception Mystery (PAGE 2)

AFTER THE VIDEO: Discuss and analyze their answers.

The most reasonable answer belongs to Character # _____ because

_____

_____

_____

_____

(Justify how this character's work makes sense.)

Let's help the others:

	Character #___:	Character #___:	Character #___:
What did this character do that was correct?			
Identify their error			
What do they need to know to understand for next time?			

298

© McCarthy Math Academy

TAKING ON THE B.E.S.T.

  **Video Lesson** | **Area and Perimeter of Composite Figures**

1 What is the area and perimeter of the composite figure?

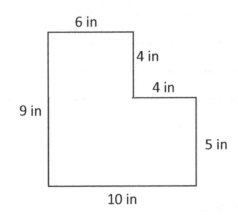

6 in
4 in
4 in
9 in
5 in
10 in

2 A school is planning to build an athletic court. A drawing of the plans is shown below. What is the area and perimeter of the athletic court design?

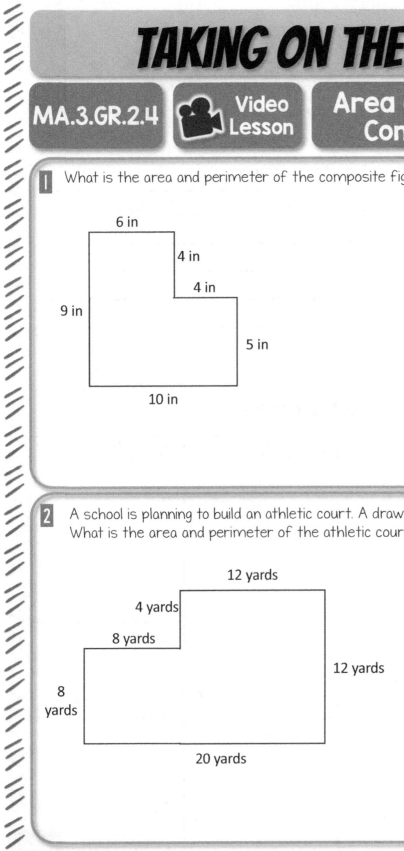

12 yards
4 yards
8 yards
12 yards
8 yards
20 yards

299

© McCarthy Math Academy

TAKING ON THE B.E.S.T.

| MA.3.GR.2.4 | Extra Practice #1 | Area and Perimeter of Composite Figures |

1 What is the area and perimeter of the composite figure?

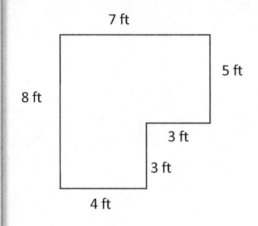

2 The first floor of the Lopez residence is shown below. What is the perimeter of the first floor, in meters? What is the area, in square meters?

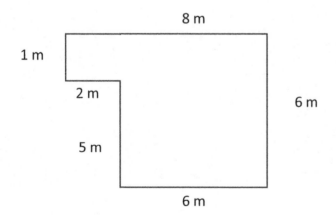

© McCarthy Math Academy

TAKING ON THE B.E.S.T.

MA.3.GR.2.4 | **Extra Practice #2** | **Area and Perimeter of Composite Figures**

1 What is the area and perimeter of the composite figure?

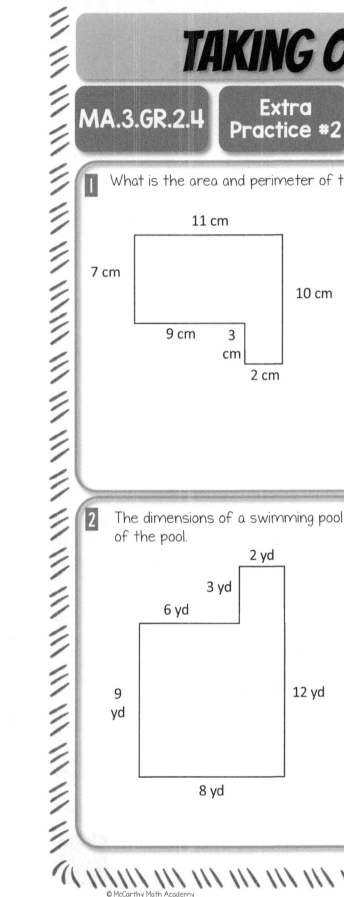

11 cm

7 cm

10 cm

9 cm

3 cm

2 cm

2 The dimensions of a swimming pool is shown below. Determine the perimeter and area of the pool.

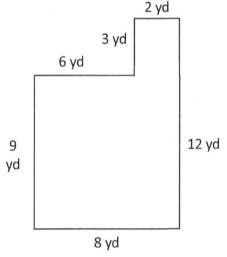

2 yd

3 yd

6 yd

9 yd

12 yd

8 yd

© McCarthy Math Academy

TAKING ON THE B.E.S.T.

| Math Missions | Area and Perimeter of Composite Figures

PART ONE

Measure and record the dimensions of the composite figure to the nearest centimeter.

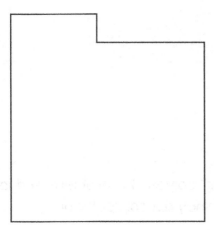

PART TWO

Determine the perimeter and area of the composite figure. Explain how you worked through each task.

_____

_____

_____

_____

_____

_____

_____

302

© McCarthy Math Academy

TAKING ON THE B.E.S.T.

BEFORE THE VIDEO: Solve the problem on your own.

What is the perimeter and area of the composite figure?

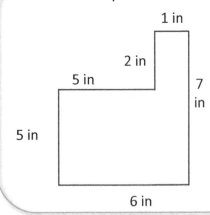

1 in

2 in

5 in

7 in

5 in

5 in

6 in

DURING THE VIDEO: Pause after each "character" solves the problem and jot down quick notes to help you remember what they did correctly or incorrectly.

Character #1 _____	Character #2 _____
Character #3 _____	**Character #4** _____

© McCarthy Math Academy

TAKING ON THE B.E.S.T.

MA.3.GR.2.4 | Math Misconception Mystery (PAGE 2)

AFTER THE VIDEO: Discuss and analyze their answers.

The most reasonable answer belongs to Character # _____ because

_____

_____

_____

_____

(Justify how this character's work makes sense.)

Let's help the others:

	Character #___:	Character #___:	Character #___:
What did this character do that was correct?			
Identify their error			
What do they need to know to understand for next time?			

© McCarthy Math Academy

TAKING ON THE B.E.S.T.

  Video Lesson | **Represent Data: Pictographs**

The third graders at Kindness Elementary collected data on their favorite color. Use the data in the table to create a pictograph to represent the data. Then, answer the questions below.

TABLE

Favorite Color	
Blue	12
Red	9
White	3
Green	8

PICTOGRAPH

Why is it important to study the key?

_____

_____

_____

_____

Describe how you determined the scale for the key.

_____

_____

_____

_____

© McCarthy Math Academy

TAKING ON THE B.E.S.T.

| **Represent Data: Pictographs**

The third graders at Integrity Elementary collected data on their favorite fruit. Use the data in the table to create a pictograph to represent the data. Then, answer the questions below.

TABLE

Favorite Fruit	
Apple	15
Banana	10
Strawberry	30
Mango	25

PICTOGRAPH

Why is it important to study the key?

_____

_____

_____

_____

Describe how you determined the scale for the key.

_____

_____

_____

_____

© McCarthy Math Academy

TAKING ON THE B.E.S.T.

 **Video Lesson**

Represent Data: Bar Graphs

The third graders at Kindness Elementary collected data on their favorite genre of music. Use the data in the table to create a vertical and horizontal bar graph to represent the data. Then, answer the questions below.

HORIZONTAL BAR GRAPH

TABLE

Favorite Genre of Music	
Pop	8
Hip Hop	5
Country	3
Classical	4

Describe how you determined the scales for the bar graphs.

_____

_____

_____

VERTICAL BAR GRAPH

If you changed the scales, how would that change the look of your bar graphs?

_____

_____

_____

307

The third graders at Integrity Elementary collected data on their favorite sport. Use the data in the table to create a vertical and horizontal bar graph to represent the data. Then, answer the questions below.

HORIZONTAL BAR GRAPH

TABLE

Favorite Sport	
Soccer	10
Football	25
Golf	15
Ice Skating	40

Describe how you determined the scales for the bar graphs.

_____

_____

_____

VERTICAL BAR GRAPH

If you changed the scales, how would that change the look of your bar graphs?

_____

_____

_____

© McCarthy Math Academy

Represent Data: Line Plots

The third graders in Mrs. Garcia's class collected data for the time they woke up on Saturday. The data they collected is shown below. Use the data to create a line plot.

LINE PLOT

Time Students Woke On Saturday	
6 a.m.	8 a.m.
8 a.m.	9 a.m.
9 a.m.	10 a.m.
7 a.m.	9 a.m.
7 a.m.	8 a.m.
7 a.m.	6 a.m.
6 a.m.	7 a.m.

←————————————————→

What do the Xs represent on this line plot?

_____

_____

At which time did most students wake up on Saturday?

_____

_____

© McCarthy Math Academy

TAKING ON THE B.E.S.T.

MA.3.DP.1.1	Extra Practice #3	Represent Data: Line Plots

The third graders in Mr. Hapner's class collected data for number of laps they walked around the track. The data they collected is shown below. Use the data to create a line plot.

LINE PLOT

Laps Walked	
3 laps	5 laps
4 laps	6 laps
3 laps	6 laps
4 laps	7 laps
3 laps	3 laps
4 laps	4 laps
5 laps	3 laps

$\longleftrightarrow$

What do the Xs represent on this line plot?

_____

_____

How many laps did most of the students walk around the track?

_____

_____

© McCarthy Math Academy

TAKING ON THE B.E.S.T.

| Math Missions | **Create and Represent Data Multiple Ways**

Roll a number cube 20 times. Record the number you roll each time in the table below. Then create a line plot using the data you collected. Include the title, labels, and units.

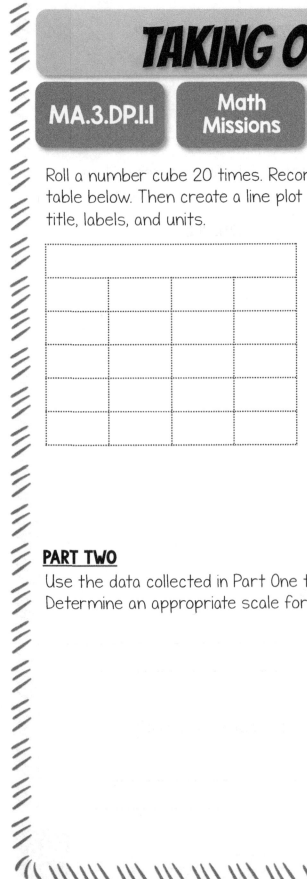

PART TWO

Use the data collected in Part One to create a bar graph and pictograph. Determine an appropriate scale for each, the title, and labels.

© McCarthy Math Academy

TAKING ON THE B.E.S.T.

Math Misconception Mystery (PAGE 1)

BEFORE THE VIDEO: Solve the problem on your own.

Bentley surveyed the minutes spent reading by the students in his class. Create a line plot that correctly displays the data that Bentley collected.

TIME SPENT READING	
10 minutes	25 minutes
15 minutes	20 minutes
15 minutes	10 minutes
20 minutes	15 minutes
10 minutes	25 minutes

DURING THE VIDEO: Pause after each "character" solves the problem and jot down quick notes to help you remember what they did correctly or incorrectly.

Character #1 _____

Character #2 _____

Character #3 _____

Character #4 _____

312

© McCarthy Math Academy

MA.3.DP.1.1	Math Misconception Mystery (PAGE 2)

AFTER THE VIDEO: Discuss and analyze their answers.

The most reasonable answer belongs to Character # _____ because

_____

_____

_____

_____

(Justify how this character's work makes sense.)

Let's help the others:

	Character #___:	Character #___:	Character #___:
What did this character do that was correct?			
Identify their error			
What do they need to know to understand for next time?			

© McCarthy Math Academy

TAKING ON THE B.E.S.T.

MA.3.DP.I.2	 Video Lesson	Interpret Data: Pictographs and Bar Graphs

Jackie surveys her classmates on their favorite mammals and reptiles, as shown in the bar graph and pictograph below.

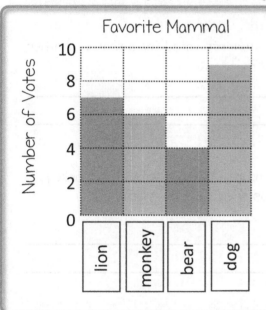

Favorite Mammal

How many students voted for their favorite mammal?

_____

_____

How many more students voted for dogs than lions as their favorite mammal?

_____

_____

Favorite Reptiles	
snake	X X X X X
iguana	X X X
turtle	X ˅
alligator	X X X ˅

KEY
X = 2 votes

How many students voted for snakes and turtles?

_____

_____

How many fewer students voted for iguanas than alligators?

_____

_____

314

TAKING ON THE B.E.S.T.

| MA.3.DP.I.2 | Extra Practice #1 | Interpret Data: Pictographs and Bar Graphs |

Eduardo surveys his students in 3rd grade on their favorite mammals and reptiles, as shown in the bar graph and pictograph below.

Favorite Mammal

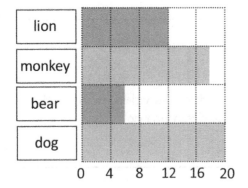

Number of Votes

How many students voted for a mammal other than a bear?

_____

_____

How many more students voted for monkeys than lions as their favorite mammal?

_____

_____

Favorite Reptiles	
snake	X X X X X X ˅
iguana	X X X X X
turtle	˅
alligator	X X X X X

KEY
X = 6 votes

How many students voted for iguanas and turtles?

_____

_____

How many fewer students voted for alligators than snakes?

_____

_____

© McCarthy Math Academy

TAKING ON THE B.E.S.T.

Kyle surveyed his classmates about their siblings, as shown in the line plot and circle graph below.

Number of Siblings

```
      x
      x
x     x
x  x  x
x  x  x
x  x  x  x        x
+--+--+--+--+--+--+--+-->
0  1  2  3  4  5  6
```

How many students have three or more siblings?

_____

What is the most common number of siblings students have in Kyle's class?

_____

How many of Kyle's classmates do not have any siblings?

_____

Type of School Siblings Attend

High School
2 siblings

Elementary School
6 siblings

Middle School
5 siblings

Preschool
8 siblings

How many siblings are in a grade other than elementary school?

_____

How many more siblings are in preschool than elementary school?

_____

© McCarthy Math Academy

| MA.3.DP.I.2 | Extra Practice #2 | Interpret Data: Line Plots and Circle Graphs |

Brianna surveyed the students at her school about their eating habits and preferences, as shown on the line plot and circle graph below.

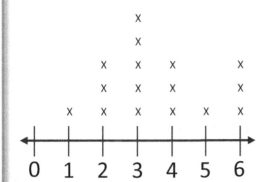

Servings of Vegetables

How many students eat exactly 2 servings of vegetables?

_____

How many students eat fewer than 4 servings of vegetables?

_____

How many students eat 3 or more servings of vegetables?

_____

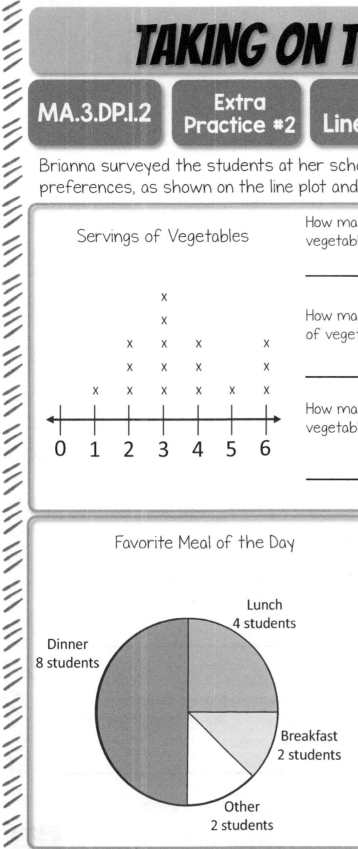

Favorite Meal of the Day

Lunch
4 students

Dinner
8 students

Breakfast
2 students

Other
2 students

How many students picked a meal other than breakfast as their favorite?

_____

How many students were surveyed?

_____

© McCarthy Math Academy

TAKING ON THE B.E.S.T.

MA.3.DP.I.2 | Math Missions | Interpret Data

A pizza shop tracks data to analyze their customers preferences.

PART ONE

Use this table to create a line plot. Then create two questions based on the data. Include an answer key.

Number of Pizzas Ordered By Top 10 Customers in March	
20	15
19	15
18	17
20	15
15	18

PART TWO

Use the data in this circle graph to create a bar graph. Then create two questions based on the data. Include an answer key.

Types of Pizzas Ordered in March

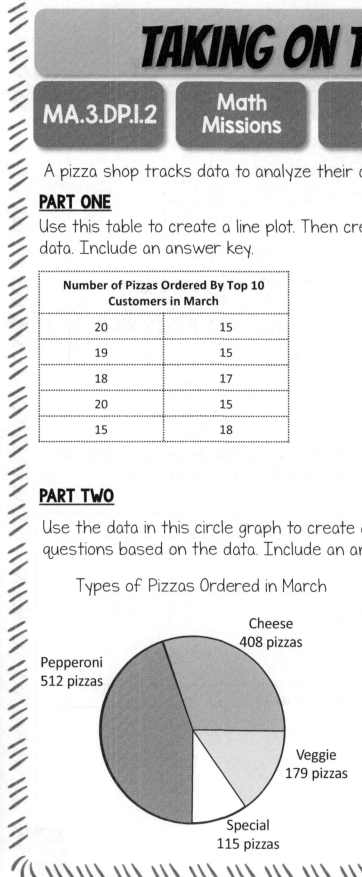

Cheese
408 pizzas

Pepperoni
512 pizzas

Veggie
179 pizzas

Special
115 pizzas

© McCarthy Math Academy

TAKING ON THE B.E.S.T.

Math Misconception Mystery
(PAGE 1)

BEFORE THE VIDEO: Solve the problem on your own.

A book store collects data based on the types of books sold. How many books were sold, not including Historical Fiction?

Books Sold	
Fantasy	X X X X
Informational Text	X X X X X ∨
Mystery	X X X X X X X X
Historical Fiction	X X X X X X

KEY
X = 10 books

DURING THE VIDEO: Pause after each "character" solves the problem and jot down quick notes to help you remember what they did correctly or incorrectly.

Character #1 _____

Character #2 _____

Character #3 _____

Character #4 _____

319

© McCarthy Math Academy

TAKING ON THE B.E.S.T.

MA.3.DP.I.2	Math Misconception Mystery (PAGE 2)

AFTER THE VIDEO: Discuss and analyze their answers.

The most reasonable answer belongs to Character # _____ because

_____

_____

_____

_____

(Justify how this character's work makes sense.)

Let's help the others:

	Character #___:	Character #___:	Character #___:
What did this character do that was correct?			
Identify their error			
What do they need to know to understand for next time?			

320

© McCarthy Math Academy

Made in the USA
Middletown, DE
04 September 2024

60043442R00179